A PROSECUTOR'S STORY

Truth, Honor, and Justice are More Than Just Words

ALAN A. COOK

TABLE OF CONTENTS

DEDICATION

I dedicate this book to my grandchildren, Claire and Elise. One day, I hope that they will read these pages and realize that their "Granddaddy" was once a real Georgia prosecutor.

INTRODUCTION

From 1987 until 2001, I served as a state criminal prosecutor in a relatively small, rural Georgia judicial circuit called the Alcovy Judicial Circuit.[1] This two-county circuit comprised of Newton and Walton Counties was located approximately 30 miles east of Atlanta. From 1990-2000, I was the Circuit's elected District Attorney – having been first elected in 1990 and subsequently re-elected in 1992 and 1996.

Newton County and its county seat, the City of Covington, are perhaps best known for the Georgia-based TV shows and movies that have been filmed there. *The Heat of the Night* starring Carrol O'Connor as Sheriff Bill Gillespie was filmed there from 1989-1995.[2] *The Dukes of Hazzard* starring John Schneider and Tom Wopat, who portrayed Bo and Luke Duke, was also filmed there. And scenes from *Cannonball Run* with Burt Reynolds were filmed there as well. More recently, the town was featured in *The Vampire Diaries* and *Sweet Magnolias*.

Walton County was named after George Walton, a signer of the Declaration of Independence and later, Governor of the state of Georgia. Walton County is also known as the site of the last mass lynching in the Old South – the Moore's Ford Lynching in 1946. Several

---

[1] The Alcovy Circuit is named after the Alcovy River that flows through each of its two counties.

[2] My wife and I once dined near O'Connor, his wife, and his son Hugh (who played Deputy Lonnie Jamison in Heat) at the Victorian House restaurant in nearby Conyers, Georgia.

1

books have been written about this sad episode in U.S. history.[3] I was the District Attorney when the investigation into this still-unsolved crime was re-opened in the 1990s. By that time, however, only a few potential suspects were still alive – and no one was talking.[4]

All told, I prosecuted for almost 14 years and tried 122 jury trials[5] before joining the faculty at the University of Georgia School of Law in 2001.[6] What follows is the true inside story of some of the shocking and sometimes bizarre cases that I grappled with while seeking justice as a Georgia prosecutor.[7] [8]

---

3 See Fire in a Canebrake: The Last Mass Lynching in America by Laura Wexler and The Last Lynching: How a Gruesome Mass Murder Rocked a Small Georgia Town by Anthony Pitch.

[4] If there had been enough evidence to charge a suspect in this case, I would have pursued it vigorously. It would have been one of the trials of the century. See Chapter 6 – Whodunit?, The Moore's Ford "Mass Lynching" Case.

[5] See Appendix A for a complete list of my jury trials and Appendix B for a complete list of my appellate cases.

[6] I served as the Director of the Prosecutorial Clinic Program (later renamed the Prosecutorial Justice Program) from 2001 until my retirement in 2019. In addition to teaching criminal law and procedure to aspiring prosecutors, I also taught a trial practice skills course. I eventually rose to the rank of Clinical Professor of Law.

[7] When I first began working on this book, I was amazed at how many details I was able to recall about cases that I had prosecuted 20+ years earlier. To supplement my memory, I relied upon newspaper articles that I had saved and included in my scrapbooks and pulled some forgotten details from the appellate briefs that I had written in these cases.

[8] NOTE: Any person named herein who was not charged with and convicted of a crime or whose conviction was subsequently reversed or set aside (and not reinstated) is presumed to be innocent.

CHAPTER 1

A Career in Prosecution

Of all the career paths that I could have chosen, why did I choose to become a criminal prosecutor? Well, I think it all started when I became interested in politics in high school and began reading about our Constitution and the Bill of Rights. Politically, I gravitated toward Libertarianism and its emphasis on individual rights and individual freedoms. That, in turn, led me to an appreciation of the ground-breaking Warren Court decisions of the 1960s that focused on the constitutional rights of individuals accused of committing crimes.[9] Could there be a more important individual right than freedom from an unlawful arrest? Or freedom from an unjust conviction premised upon unreliable or illegally seized evidence?

So, why not pursue a career as a criminal defense attorney, you might ask? Good question. When I was growing up, most of the TV shows, movies, and books celebrated the criminal defense attorney as the hero of the criminal justice system. For example, has there ever been a more heroic figure in literature than Atticus Finch in *To Kill a Mockingbird*? And what about television's Perry Mason? In these

---

[9] See, e.g., Mapp v. Ohio, 367 U.S. 643 (1961); Gideon v. Wainwright, 372 U.S. 335 (1963); Brady v. Maryland, 373 U.S. 83 (1963); Miranda v. Arizona, 384 U.S. 436 (1966); and Katz v. U.S., 389 U.S. 347 (1967).

fictional stories, the criminal justice system was usually depicted as a critically flawed system in which the cards were almost always stacked against the (wrongfully accused) defendant. But the more I studied it in college and law school, the more I came to realize that the criminal justice system in the United States – with a few notable exceptions[10] – worked quite well. In fact, I learned that the American criminal justice system was the envy of the world.

My studies also persuaded me that, contrary to popular literary and on-screen memes, prosecutors in our system of criminal justice have far more power to affect outcomes and to "do justice" than criminal defense attorneys. Between the two, only prosecutors are legally and ethically obligated to protect the rights of *both* crime victims *and* defendants.[11] It seemed to me, therefore, that what our system needed most was a greater emphasis on educating, hiring, training, and retaining top-notch prosecutors. And more to the point, it needed the kind of prosecutors who were willing to objectively assess the merits of each case in order to screen out bad or weak cases – for justice in our criminal justice system depends, first and foremost, upon the wise use of prosecutorial power.

So, long before prosecutors received their just due in TV shows like *Law & Order* in the 1990s, I set my sights on becoming a prosecutor.[12]

---

[10] The exceptions, of course, would include inter alia the disparate treatment of indigent and minority defendants – particularly in the decades preceding the Warren Court decisions of the 1960s.

[11] See ABA Model Rules of Professional Conduct, Rule 3.8, Special Responsibilities of a Prosecutor.

[12] If you are a "true crime" junkie and aren't interested in my backstory, you can skip to Chapter 2 now.

The Path to Prosecution

I grew up in a traditional middle-class family in Conyers, Georgia. I was the middle son of an insurance agent and a homemaker. My parents had each attended but not completed college. My father's college career was interrupted by his service in the Navy during the Korean War. And my mother worked for AT&T until his tour of duty was over. Afterward, they started a family and had to place earning an income ahead of earning their college degrees. I think this explains, in part, why my parents prioritized a college education for their three boys over fancy cars and expensive vacations. If so, they achieved their goal for all three of their children not only graduated from college, but also earned post-graduate degrees (including a Ph.D. in Physics, a Juris Doctor Degree, and a Master's in Education).

My childhood was relatively uneventful. I loved Major League Baseball, collecting baseball cards, and playing Little League baseball. I was even selected as an All-Star one year. And another year, my team won the League Championship. (One of my other teams, however, finished 0-13.) I was a very studious kid. I completed high school with the highest grade point average in my class of over 400 students and was our graduation speaker. Following my graduation from Rockdale County High School in 1977, I attended Oxford College of Emory University (earning an A.A. Degree in 1979). I transferred to the University of Georgia where I completed my college education (earning a B.A. in Political Science in 1981). I then earned my J.D. from the University of Georgia School of Law in 1984. I met my future wife, Debra, at Oxford College and we got married after my second year of law school.

After graduating from law school, I moved to Augusta, Georgia, where Debra was completing her last year of dental school at the

Medical College of Georgia. Knowing that we would be moving back toward our home towns of Conyers and Covington upon her graduation, I low-balled my salary requirements and was quickly hired as a junior associate by the Augusta firm of Nixon, Yow, Waller, & Capers. I spent most of that year researching and drafting memoranda for the senior partners – one of whom was the City Attorney for the City of Augusta. Upon Debra's graduation, we moved to Conyers where she started her own dental practice, and I began a two-year judicial clerkship with the Honorable Thomas W. Ridgway, Chief Judge of Superior Courts in the Alcovy Judicial Circuit. My son, Philip, was born during my last year with the judge.

During my judicial clerkship, in addition to drafting most of the judge's civil orders and summary judgments, I was able to acquaint myself with the Alcovy Circuit and its legal community. And as a result, upon leaving Judge Ridgway's employ, I joined the Law Office of Samuel D. Ozburn in Covington, Georgia. Mr. Ozburn – known to just about everyone in Covington as "Sammy" – was a very well-respected solo practitioner who had a general civil practice. I quickly discovered, however, that civil practice wasn't the right fit for me. My "Type A" personality hungered for a narrower field of law – something that I could learn thoroughly and master quickly.

When Brenda Hitchcock, the lead secretary in the Newton County District Attorney's Office, alerted me to a vacant assistant district attorney (ADA) position in the Walton County District Attorney's Office, I jumped at the chance to become a prosecutor. I interviewed with District Attorney John M. Ott and was soon hired. At that time, the District Attorney's Office in the Alcovy Circuit only had two ADAs – one in Newton County and one in Walton County. Thus, I was the only ADA in the Walton County Courthouse. So, with the exception of the cases that District Attorney Ott chose to handle himself, every criminal case in Walton County was my responsibility to prosecute. Pretty heady stuff for a 28-year-old, relatively inexperienced attorney.[13] But it was a great learning experience, and I felt like I was making a real contribution to my community and to my profession. Frankly, I would have been perfectly content to serve in that role for many years to come. But as fate would have it, the opportunity for advancement presented itself early. Very early.

Seeking Public Office

After serving as an ADA for just over two years, my world changed dramatically when District Attorney Ott was appointed to fill a vacancy on the Alcovy Circuit Superior Court bench. As a result, Ott's unexpired term in office would need to be filled by a non-partisan Special Election. While the state of Georgia made arrangements to hold this Special Election, Ott's Chief Assistant in Newton County, Miles Wilson,[14] would serve as the "Acting" Alcovy Circuit District Attorney. Wilson and I had rarely crossed paths in the two years that I had worked in the DA's Office – typically only when we would travel to each other's assigned county to assist one another at trial terms. Nonetheless, these infrequent encounters allowed me to get to know both Wilson and the staff in the Newton County DA's Office fairly well.

Once Ott was officially sworn in as a Superior Court judge, a mad scramble to replace him commenced. Wilson was the first to announce his intention to run for Ott's unexpired term. Two experienced local attorneys, John Degonia and Charles Day, soon followed suit. But before long, many of the staff members in both the Walton

---

[13] I actually orally argued a murder case in the Georgia Supreme Court before I tried my first jury trial! (District Attorney Ott who had tried this case months earlier had a conflict that day and asked me to go in his place.) See Williams v. State, 258 Ga. 80 (1988).

[14] Not his real name.

and Newton offices encouraged me to run. I also received encouragement to run from several members of the Walton County Bar. And perhaps most gratifying, many of the Walton County police officers that I had worked with for several years urged me to run as well.

Was I ready? Although I had entertained the thought of becoming a district attorney *someday*, I had never imagined that that day might come so soon. After all, I was only 31 years old. And I had only been an ADA for less than three years. On the other hand, I was confident in my ability to try cases. In fact, I had successfully tried my last twelve jury trials. Nonetheless, I couldn't help but feel that public office was seeking me rather than me seeking it. But I knew that if I hesitated and patiently waited my turn, the opportunity might not present itself again for a long, long time – if ever. Thus, after some soul-searching, I decided to toss my hat into the ring. There were now four candidates in the race.

Now that I had made my decision, one big obstacle still stood in my way: I didn't live in the Alcovy Circuit – a prerequisite to seeking this constitutional office. I lived in neighboring Rockdale County. To make matters worse, my family and I had only lived in our first "starter home" for a little more than one year. Moving again so soon was a lot to ask of my family. But my wife, Debra, recognizing that this might be a once in a lifetime opportunity for me, was all in. And my son, Philip, who was just three years old, was probably too young to voice an objection.[15] So, we put our house on the market and started looking for a place to live in the Alcovy Circuit.

Unfortunately, with the Special Election looming on the horizon, I didn't have much time to find an ideal place to move my family.

---

[15] Actually, if asked, Philip probably would have expressed an opinion. As my law school classmate and good friend Howard Rothbloom once observed, even at age 3, Philip had a phenomenal vocabulary and spoke like a "little adult."

Thus, we ended up renting a small, bug-infested house in Covington. I changed my voter registration, bought a cot, and began sleeping in this house just two days *prior* to filing my qualifying fee. Debra and Philip, along with some of our furniture, kitchen supplies, and clothes, soon followed. Life in the "bughouse" was unpleasant, but we did what we had to do. And fortunately, our stay there would be a short one.

The race was on. In 90 days, the Alcovy Circuit would have a new District Attorney. In the meantime, Wilson and I reached a "gentleman's agreement" that he would run the Newton Office, and I would run the Walton Office. If he won, he'd keep me as one of his ADAs. If I won, I'd keep him. Before long, however, our relationship soured. I made a point of never mentioning Wilson's name in my campaign ads and literature. I ran strictly on my qualifications and record. But several of his ads *did* mention me – and not in a favorable light. In particular, he ran a full-page newspaper ad attacking me as being an outsider from neighboring Rockdale County.[16] This attack ignored the fact that given my two-year stint as Judge Ridgway's law clerk, I had actually worked in the Alcovy Circuit as long as, if not longer than, he had. Wilson's campaign tactics would eventually force me to make another difficult decision.

I was a Political Science major in college, but I had never actually participated in a political campaign. Nonetheless, I thoroughly enjoyed designing my campaign materials, slogans, and strategy.[17] Given the fact that I still had a full-time job and had little time to knock on doors,

---

[16] In Wilson's ad, he placed a photo of his house in Newton County next to a photo of my house in Rockdale County. And underneath the photo of my house, but not his, was the street address. Many of my family's personal belongings were still in that now-unoccupied house. His ad, therefore, was akin to an open invitation to burglars and thieves to "come and get it." Worse, he attacked my motives in seeking public office in the Alcovy Circuit. He claimed that I was only interested in grabbing the pay increase the job would bring. That was beyond the pale.

[17] My wife's Aunt Helen Parker designed my campaign logo.

I decided to focus primarily on newspaper ads and mailouts. This was not cheap – especially on a young prosecutor's meager state salary. And because I was hesitant to ask for campaign contributions, my campaign was largely self-financed.[18] In the process, I nearly exhausted whatever "life savings" I had up to that point.

And I had to face another reality. Sadly, the general public doesn't really know what a district attorney does and rarely bothers to research the candidates' qualifications before voting. To make matters worse, I only had 90 days to try to convince them that I was the best choice for the job. But how? In my mailouts, I was able to boast of having "won"[19] my last twelve jury trials. And the campaign photographs of my family were endearing.[20] But would that be enough? Fortunately, my campaign received a big boost when I was endorsed by the Police Benevolent Association.[21] Having the support of the Circuit's police officers would send a powerful message to the electorate. And then, perhaps of even greater significance, I was endorsed just five days before the Special Election by the Editorial Board of the *Covington News*.[22]

---

[18] My campaign Treasurer was my father-in-law, Willie Parker. Willie was an invaluable asset to my campaign – a true DIY enthusiast. He helped me paint my unconventional plywood campaign signs and helped me place them at key intersections throughout the two-county Circuit. He even placed one of the larger signs on posts in his backyard facing the morning traffic on Interstate 20

[19] I use this term reluctantly here. As I would later tell my law students, a prosecutor (and society) "wins" whenever justice is done. Thus, there are occasions when an acquittal is a "win."

[20] My wife and son were great campaigners. Debra made us sweatshirts with my campaign logo stenciled across the front. We would wear our matching sweatshirts and hand out my campaign literature at high school football games, fall festivals, and political BBQs. Philip had the routine down pat. He'd go up to strangers, hand them a campaign pamphlet, and say, "Vote for my Daddy."

[21] Wilson attacked this too, asking, "Why is Alan Cook their [the police officers'] fair-haired boy?"

[22] The endorsement read: Alan Cook strikes us as the individual best equipped to manage the heavy caseloads in both counties in this circuit. He also strikes us as the candidate with the experience to prosecute important cases in the two counties, as well as provide the strong leadership required in the two courthouses. By all accounts, Cook is the candidate who will be able to

And then came the moment of truth. On Election Day, of the four candidates, I garnered the most votes – a plurality, but short of the required majority vote.[23] Soon thereafter, however, the second and third-place finishers, Mr. Degonia and Mr. Day, announced their intentions to withdraw from the race. Both cited the significantly higher vote totals that I had received in the first round of voting. But the fourth-place finisher, i.e., the candidate finishing in last place, Mr. Wilson, refused to concede. So, despite the fact that I had received over twice as many votes as Wilson had, there would have to be a runoff.

I knew from my political science background that runoffs could be tricky. Would my supporters return to the polls? Fortunately, they did, and on the day following the runoff election, the newspaper headline in the *Covington News* read: "Cook Swamps Wilson with 71% of the Vote." This headline will never be as famous as "Dewey Defeats Truman"– but it will always be *my* favorite headline. To me, this headline was vindication for all the negative ads that Wilson had run against me.

After a whirlwind campaign, I had been elected as the new District Attorney for the Alcovy Judicial Circuit – one of only 49 elected district attorneys in the state of Georgia. And on November 30, 1990 (my wife's 31st birthday), I was sworn in at the State Capitol in front of family and friends. At age 31, I was the youngest district attorney in the state of Georgia. As the late, great Chicago Cubs sportscaster Harry Caray would say, "Holy cow!"

---

work best with law enforcement agencies in Newton and Walton Counties – a vital quality for a successful district attorney. The Covington News endorses ALAN COOK for Alcovy Circuit District Attorney.

[23] The vote totals were: Cook (5,275 – 38.8%); Degonia (3,031-22.3%); Day (2,753-20.2%); Wilson (2,545-18.7%).

Assembling the Team

Then came the task of governing.

What to do about Wilson? In my mind, Wilson had breached our gentlemen's agreement by his conduct during the campaign. So, on the day after the election, I placed a note in Wilson's office chair. It read something like this: "Resign or be fired." To his credit, he accepted his dismissal in stride and became one of the better criminal defense attorneys in town. I came to admire how he zealously represented his clients. And although I can't say that we were ever friends thereafter, we worked well together in the years that followed.

My next decision was an easy one: I retained the entire staff of administrative assistants, secretaries, and investigators in both the Newton County and Walton County offices. But I still needed to appoint two new assistant district attorneys – one to replace Wilson and the other to replace me. For my Chief ADA, I appointed Ken Wynne. Up to that point in time, Wynne had been our Circuit's Child Support Recovery ADA. Fortunately, Ott had given Ken the opportunity to try some cases in Superior Court where he had demonstrated great potential – and then some. One down.[24]

Next, I made a concerted effort to appoint a black ADA. In the history of the Alcovy Circuit, there had never been a black ADA. I felt that if I could hire a black ADA, it would send a powerful message to the Black community that my office would not ignore their concerns. I had my eye on a young attorney by the name of Eric Morrow. I had come to know and like Morrow when he practiced law with local attorney

---

[24] Wynne would later succeed me as District Attorney in 2001, and in 2010, he was appointed to the Alcovy Superior Court bench.

Horace Johnson.[25] By this time, however, Morrow had secured a job with the Dekalb County Solicitor's Office. To lure Morrow away from that office, I would need to convince the Newton County Commission to authorize a salary increase. And they did. Soon thereafter, the first black ADA in the history of the Circuit was on board.[26]

In the years that followed, my allotment of ADAs increased from just two to over eight. Nonetheless, I had to periodically replace ADAs who left seeking higher-paying ADA jobs in Metro Atlanta or more lucrative jobs in private practice. It was a bittersweet part of my job. I hated to see them go, but I was happy to see them advancing in their legal careers. In fact, as of the writing of this book, five have become judges.

This turnover in ADAs also afforded me the opportunity to appoint the Circuit's first female ADAs with trial responsibilities. Mary Diversi Hanks, who served as an ADA in Walton County, was the first of many. Anne Templeton LaMalva, who I later named Senior ADA in charge of the Walton office, was one of my longest-serving ADAs. Jennifer Greene Ammons, who served as an ADA in the Newton office for many years, later became General Counsel for the Department of Driver Services before becoming General Counsel for the Department of Corrections. I also appointed Vanessa Webber to become our first full-time Juvenile Court ADA – a position that she still holds at the time of this writing. And my last female ADA appointment, Layla

---

[25] Johnson and my wife, Debra, had gone to high school together in Newton County. He would later become a Superior Court judge in the Alcovy Circuit

[26] Unfortunately, I soon discovered that my rural Circuit could not compete with the lure of Atlanta for talented black lawyers. Before long, Morrow left to join the Law Department for the City of Atlanta. And a second attempt years later to hire and retain a black ADA produced similar results.

Zon, would later succeed Wynne as the Alcovy Circuit's first female District Attorney in 2010.

Too Young?

Did I mention that I was the youngest district attorney in the state of Georgia when I was first elected? Well, that led to some funny and awkward moments over the years. One incident, in particular, stands out in my memory. In the Willie Frank Williams case,[27] both of the Alcovy judges had to recuse themselves when a man named Echols confessed that he, not Williams, had committed a rape for which Williams had been convicted years earlier.[28] Judge John Ruffin from the Augusta Circuit was named to preside over Echols' preliminary hearing.[29] Given the high-profile nature of this case, I decided to handle this hearing myself.

Following the hearing in the Magistrate Court Annex, I approached the bench to thank Judge Ruffin for making the two-hour drive from Augusta to Monroe, and the conversation that ensued sounded something like this:

> Judge Ruffin: *Mr. Cook, would you take me over to the Courthouse so I can meet the DA while I'm here?*
>
> Cook: *Well, your Honor, actually, I am the District Attorney.*
>
> Judge Ruffin: *Noooo! You're too young!*
>
> Cook: *So I've been told, Your Honor.*

---

[27] See Chapter 5 – Prosecutorial Discretion, The Willie Frank Williams Case.

[28] Judge Sorrells had represented Williams, and Judge Ott had prosecuted him – so both had to recuse themselves from handling the case.

[29] Ruffin would later become a judge on the Georgia Court of Appeals.

Seeking Re-Election

In 1992, after just a little over two years in office, I had to run for a full 4-year term. Fortunately, I had no opposition. Running unopposed for office was a delight. Unlike the Special Election two years earlier, other than having to pay the qualifying fee, I didn't have to dig into my own pockets to fund my campaign. And on Election night, I didn't have to go to bed wondering if I'd have a job when I woke up the next morning. Running unopposed? I highly recommend it. Unfortunately, in 1996, I would not be so lucky.

Remember my statement about the general public and its ignorance and disinterest in district attorney races? Well, the 1996 election was a prime example. By 1996, I had been a prosecutor for over eight years and had a solid record of securing convictions in major cases, including a successful death penalty prosecution. My opponent was a man named Stan Cox. Cox had been an assistant solicitor (misdemeanor prosecutor) years earlier in another Circuit, had a small-town private practice, and dabbled in criminal defense work. Although I'm admittedly biased, I don't think that a side-by-side comparison of our experience and qualifications was a close call. But, as with most such elections, the result would ultimately be determined, not by such objective criteria, but by whether an "R" or a "D" appeared next to our names on the ballot.

How could that be, you ask? Well, although the Special Election in 1990 had been a non-partisan election, in 1992, I was forced to declare a political party affiliation when I qualified to run for re-election. At that time, *all* of the elected officials in the Alcovy Circuit were Democrats. In my estimation, even though my political philosophy was more closely aligned with the Republican Party than the Democrat Party, it would have been political suicide to run as a Republican.[30] So, I felt compelled by self-interest to declare as a Democrat.

By 1996, however, Georgia's political landscape was changing. The Republican Party was beginning to catch up with the Democrat majority in the Georgia General Assembly. And in Walton County, the Republican Party had become very competitive – so much so that many of the Democrat officials in Walton County had switched parties. Newton County, on the other hand, was still a Democrat stronghold. After wrestling with the pros and cons of switching parties, I reluctantly decided to declare again as a Democrat. And it darn near cost me the election.

On Election Day, Cox, who had declared as a Republican, carried Walton County, and I carried Newton County. The election would come down to the tabulation of the absentee ballots. After a very, very long night, I barely eked out a victory with 50.7% of the Circuit-wide vote. My officemates and I had dodged a bullet. Nonetheless, my victory felt more like a defeat. It was a feeling that I never wanted to experience again.

Bowing Out Gracefully

As the year 2000 approached, I began to weigh my options and assess my chances of winning a fourth term. My 1996 re-election night experience had made a lasting impression on me – and it wasn't a pleasant memory. I didn't want to put myself, my family, or my officemates through that again. So, I would either have to switch political parties (and face the inevitable "party-switcher" label), run again as a Democrat

---

[30] I was and am a fiscal conservative and a social moderate and would probably best be described in political terms as a Libertarian. But frankly, I don't like political labels. I prefer to call myself an Individualist – a follower of the political philosophy of the great 19th-century English writer and politician John Stuart Mill. His greatest work, On Liberty, is one of my favorite books.

and campaign more aggressively, or step aside. I describe some of the considerations that drove my ultimate decision below.

My son, Philip, was about to begin high school. If I ran for re-election and won a fourth term, he would be in college by the time my term was over. I really wanted to spend more time with him while he still lived at home.[31] Moreover, Philip was a trumpet player and was just getting started in high school marching band. I knew that this was going to involve a lot of nights and weekends – and I wanted to be there.[32]

And did I really have anything left to prove? After over 12 years as a prosecutor, I had done just about everything a prosecutor could do. I had won three elections. I had successfully tried many murder and death penalty cases. I had appeared before the Georgia Supreme Court and Court of Appeals on several occasions. Maybe it was time to try something new.

And if I ran again and lost to Mr. Cox, who had made it clear that he would run again, all of my officemates would face an uncertain future. All of the policies and priorities that I had worked so hard to adopt and maintain might be changed overnight by a newly-elected district attorney coming in from "the outside."

So, I decided not to run.

I let my Chief Assistant, Ken Wynne, know about my decision early on so he could make preparations to declare his candidacy – as a Republican. I told him that he would have my full support. We had

---

[31] My DA years required me to work at least a half-day every Sunday. And although I always ate weeknight dinners and spent all day on Saturdays with my family, I wanted more free weekends to spend exclusively with them.

[32] Philip's high school marching band was really good. They won first place in several state and regional band festivals. Philip would later march for the Clemson Tiger marching band for five years, was one of the trumpet line leaders, and earned a letter jacket.

worked together side-by-side for 10 years. I knew that he could build upon *our* shared past successes. And I was absolutely confident in his ability to be a great district attorney. He was a rock-solid attorney whose trial successes equaled – if not exceeded – my own. Moreover, he was well-respected and liked by the office staff and the attorneys in the local Bar.

When I made my plans known, it took many by surprise. After all, I was walking away from a prestigious high-profile job. Historically, district attorneys and sheriffs in Georgia, once elected, often served for life. But times were changing, and incumbency was no longer a guarantee of job security.[33]

Although I was very comfortable with my decision not to seek re-election, I decided to use my public platform to denounce Georgia's preposterous statutory mandate that required candidates for the office of District Attorney to run on a partisan ticket. I argued that district attorneys, like judges – who had run in nonpartisan races for decades – should be above politics. I received both praise and criticism for my stance.[34] Unfortunately, as of the writing of this book, this aspect of Georgia election law remains unchanged. And as a result, many extraordinary district attorneys have been kicked out of office simply because they chose to run under the "wrong" party label.

Fortunately for my officemates and the citizens of Newton and Walton Counties, Wynne defeated Cox in the Republican Primary

---

[33] Just four years later, for example, the outstanding long-term DA of Clayton County Bob Keller was unseated by a relative newcomer with scant qualifications for the office. (She was herself turned out four years later.)

[34] My stance was featured in a front-page story in the state's legal newspaper, the Daily Report.

and would become the next District Attorney of the Alcovy Judicial Circuit.[35]

Transitioning to Academia

As my final year in office was nearing an end, I asked District Attorney-elect Wynne if he would be willing to allow me to serve as one of his ADAs while I contemplated my next career move. He graciously agreed. I let him know, however, that despite my prosecutorial experience, I did not want him to name me as his Chief ADA. He needed the freedom to build his own team. So, for the first time in 10 years, effective January 1, 2001, I was once again a "line prosecutor"[36] with my own assigned judge and caseload.[37]

I was truly excited about my new ADA position. But as things turned out, I would only serve in this new role for seven months. Regardless, those seven months were very rewarding. They gave me the opportunity to re-live my ADA days – drafting charging documents, conducting preliminary hearings, working up plea recommendations, and running arraignment calendars. I could easily have stayed and prosecuted for several more years, but I soon got an offer that I couldn't refuse – an offer that was years in the making.

Years earlier, shortly after my election to office in 1990, I contacted the Director of the Prosecutorial Clinic Program at the University of Georgia School of Law about the possibility of securing

---

[35] Wynne served as District Attorney from 2001-2010 before his appointment to the Superior Court bench.

[36] See Chapter 15 – A Team Approach (defining "line prosecutors").

[37] Ironically, I tried a death penalty case in my very first month after returning to the office as an ADA. See Chapter 10 – Death Penalty Cases, the Brian "Chico" Terrell Case.

the services of a third-year law student to intern in my office.[38] As a result, throughout my tenure as District Attorney, many third-year law students interned in my office under Georgia's Third Year Practice Act. I thoroughly enjoyed acting as a mentor to these interns. And because I got to know my interns and their abilities well, I extended three of them offers to become ADAs in my office following their graduation from law school – Jennifer Greene Ammons, Jeff Foster, and Brian Deutsch. When in later years, however, my law student interns began to share with me their disappointment in the way the internship program was being run, I began making subtle (and not so subtle) inquiries regarding the Law School's future plans for the Prosecutorial Clinic Program.

Beginning in the Fall of 2000, I began corresponding with the Dean and Associate Dean of the Law School. And in the Summer of 2001, I received a phone call from Dean David Shipley inviting me to interview for the Program's then-vacant Directorship position.[39] Following that interview, I was offered the job, and I gleefully accepted. This was my dream job. It would allow me to impart my knowledge about prosecution to "the next generation of aspiring prosecutors"[40] and would give me the flexibility to spend more time at home with my family.

---

[38] I had participated in the Prosecutorial Clinic Program when I was a student at UGA Law in the early 1980s and had interned in the Athens-Clarke County DA's Office.

[39] The deans were also apparently aware of the students' complaints regarding the direction of the Program and had finally decided that a change in leadership was needed.

[40] Little did I know how prophetic that phrase would be. Upon my retirement in 2019, I had taught exactly 18 graduating classes – an entire generation of new prosecutors.

Training the Next Generation of Prosecutors

I joined the faculty at UGA Law as the Director of the Prosecutorial Clinic Program (later renamed the Prosecutorial Justice Program) in August of 2001. My initial challenge was to create a more academically challenging three-semester classroom component to supplement the existing two-semester third-year externship component. So, over the course of the next year and a half, I researched and prepared weekly two-hour lectures on select Georgia criminal law and procedure topics. By the time I was finished, I had created over 42 such lectures on varied topics like the investigation of crimes, the law of arrests, drafting accusations and indictments, preliminary hearings, arraignments, plea bargaining, jury trials, and appeals. And then, every year thereafter, I would research and update my lectures to keep them current.[41]

My ultimate goal for the Program was twofold: (1) to create a classroom and externship course that would enable UGA law graduates to stand out when compared to other law school graduates when applying for prosecutor jobs, and (2) to provide Georgia's district attorneys with top-notch new hires who were ready "to hit the ground running." The anecdotal evidence appears to show that I realized my goal. Of the approximately 450 students in the Program in my 18 years as its Director, I can account for over 175 who landed prosecutor jobs following graduation – including three who later became elected district attorneys and three who later became elected solicitors-general.[42]

---

[41] I eventually compiled these lectures into book form and self-published my Cook's Field Guide to Prosecution in Georgia which at the time of this writing is in its 2nd Edition.

[42] Shalena Cook Jones (J.D. '02), District Attorney in the Eastern Judicial Circuit; Todd Hayes (J.D. '02), Solicitor-General in Cherokee County; Shannon Glover Wallace (J.D. '02), District Attorney in the Blue Ridge Circuit; Joseph Cushner (J.D. '10), Solicitor-General in Bulloch County; Marie Greene Broder (J.D. '10), District Attorney in the Griffin Circuit; Charles Brooks (J.D. '11), Solicitor-General in Clayton County.

My teaching position at UGA Law also allowed me the time to pursue another passion – training child abuse professionals. In 2004, I was invited to join the faculty of *Finding Words*, a nationally recognized 5-day course for child abuse professionals that teaches about the dynamics of child sexual abuse, the proper methods for conducting child forensic interviews, and the legal prerequisites for successfully prosecuting a child molestation case. As of this writing, I am still involved in this course, which is now known as *ChildFirst*.[43] Moreover, since 2010, I have authored an annual update on the law of prosecuting child sexual abuse cases titled *CMBrief© A Comprehensive Trial Brief for Prosecuting Child Sexual Abuse Cases in Georgia*.[44]

Academia also provided me with the opportunity to try my hand at scholarly writing. Prof. Julian Cook (no relation) invited me to co-author a book with him. Together, we wrote *Adjudicative Criminal Procedure, What Matters and Why?* published by Wolters Kluwer in 2016. And after completing that book, I wrote and self-published a second book in 2018, now in its 2nd Edition, titled *Cook's Field Guide to Prosecution in Georgia* which I sell to prosecutors across Georgia.[45] My *Field Guide* has also been used as a textbook at UGA Law and the Georgia State University College of Law.

---

[43] I was commissioned by the Office of the Child Advocate to create an advanced version of this course in 2006. This course titled Advanced ChildFirst – Your Role in the Judicial Process concentrates on the investigative and testimonial phases of a child sexual abuse case. Since 2007, I have hosted this 3-day mock trial course each summer at the UGA Law campus.

[44] This publication is free to child abuse professionals and is available by contacting me at acook@uga.edu .

[45] The 2nd Edition of this publication and is available for sale by contacting me at cooksfieldguide@gmail.com .

Retirement

In June of 2019, after 35 years as a lawyer, prosecutor, and law professor, I retired from full-time teaching. I continue to write and I occasionally teach. I enjoy pickleball, hiking, reading, traveling, cheering for my Georgia Bulldogs and Atlanta Braves, and being "Granddaddy" to two special girls, Claire and Elise.

CHAPTER 2

Crimes Against Children

In the 1980s, many people were skeptical when children stepped forward to make claims of sexual abuse. Some of this skepticism stemmed from the so-called "Daycare Cases" that had exposed the dangers of using improper interviewing techniques when questioning children, e.g., the use of suggestive questions, multiple interviews of children by multiple interviewers, etc.[46] As a result, many prosecutors were hesitant to try child sexual abuse cases in the absence of strong corroborating physical or medical evidence. Unfortunately, because such corroborating evidence is rarely present in these cases, it permitted many sexual predators to escape prosecution – and to harm other children.

To overcome the investigative deficiencies exposed in the 1980s, the science of child forensic interviewing emerged in the 1990s. Experts in the field of child psychology developed research-based interviewing techniques to reduce the risk that children might misreport allegations of sexual abuse. These new and improved techniques included the use of non-leading questions,[47] conducting such interviews in a

---

[46] See, e.g., the McMartin Preschool Case in California (circa 1983), the Kelley Michaels Case in New Jersey (circa 1985), and the Little Rascals Daycare Case in North Carolina (circa 1989).

[47] For example, a trained forensic interviewer might ask, "What happened next? (Answer: "He took off my shirt."). Not "Did he take off your shirt?"(Answer: "Yes.").

child-friendly environment,[48] eliminating the practice of "confirmatory bias,"[49] and by avoiding the "negative stereotyping" of suspects.[50] These interviewing techniques – collectively referred to as interviewing "protocols" – were then taught to specially trained child forensic interviewers enabling them to elicit more accurate and detailed accounts of child sexual abuse. As a result, these child interviews came to be viewed as more objective and truth-seeking in nature. Thus, more and more prosecutors became willing to take these cases to trial – even in the absence of physical or medical evidence to corroborate the child's account of abuse.

I was one of those prosecutors. In fact, the prosecution of child sexual abuse cases became my niche. Why? Because unlike so many other crimes, the victims of child sexual abuse were *always* innocent and truly deserving of society's protection – including mine. I recount a few of my more memorable child sexual abuse cases below.

The David Huggins Case[51]

I tried my first child molestation case in 1989. The victim was a 9-year-old boy who lived with his alcoholic father. Unfortunately, the boy's father permitted a drifter by the name of David Huggins to live with them, and worse, to sleep in the boy's bedroom. Before long, Huggins began to engage in classic "grooming" techniques to gain the boy's trust

---

[48] The creation of so-called "Child Advocacy Centers" or "CACs" enabled trained professionals to interview children in a safe, non-threatening atmosphere away from the police station.

[49] Confirmatory bias involves the interviewer's assumption that (1) a child has in fact been abused, and (2) that a particular individual is the one who abused the child. This lack of objectivity may inadvertently influence a child and cause him or her to adopt the interviewer's assumptions – whether true or not.

[50] When an interviewer speaks in a derogatory manner about an alleged perpetrator, it may encourage a child to wrongfully accuse that person or to exaggerate the extent of his or her abuse.

[51] Huggins v. State, 192 Ga. App. 820 (1989).

– watching TV with him, taking him to the store, and buying him candy and gifts. Then, he proceeded to molest the boy several times a week for several months. Eventually, the boy summoned the courage to tell someone about the abuse, and Huggins was arrested and charged with child molestation.

Unfortunately, because there was no corroborating physical or medical evidence in this case, it looked like this was going to be a classic "he said, he said" case. In other words, exactly the kind of case that might not have been prosecuted in the 1980s. Fortunately, however, we located a second victim whose allegations of child abuse against Huggins had never been prosecuted. The second victim – a 16-year-old boy – had accused Huggins of molestation years earlier when the boy was only 8 years old. This was the corroborating testimony that we needed.[52] Having the advantage of hearing the testimony of *both* boys, the jury was able to "break the tie" and found Huggins guilty. And Judge Marvin Sorrells, nicknamed "Maximum Marvin" for his penchant for imposing the maximum sentence authorized by law, sentenced Huggins to life in prison.

I found the Huggins case to be the most satisfying of my fledgling career as a prosecutor. Although I had successfully tried several cases at that point, most were drug sale cases. Yes, it was great to hold drug dealers accountable for their illegal conduct. But unlike the victims of child abuse, the purchasers of illegal drugs were not truly innocent – they were willing customers.[53] Moreover, for every drug dealer I

---

[52] There is almost always a second victim – and sadly, often many other victims. People who molest children may abuse dozens if not hundreds of children before they are caught – if they are ever caught. This is why child abuse investigators are taught to always look for other victims to corroborate a child victim's story.

[53] Society, of course, was a true victim of these illegal drug sales. Myriad problems stem from illegal drug sales – addiction, family turmoil, and drug turf wars, to name a few. I might add that not all of my homicide victims were "innocent" either. Many had placed themselves in harm's way

helped send to prison, it seemed like two more stepped forward to take his place. And the drug dealers who did go to prison were soon paroled and back on the streets selling drugs. The Parole Board, however, was much less likely to grant early parole to child molesters. In fact, as of the writing of this book – over thirty years later, Huggins is still in prison![54]

After trying the Huggins case, I resolved to make the prosecution of child sexual abuse cases my specialty, i.e., to become a "Special Victims Prosecutor." In fact, even after becoming the elected District Attorney, I continued to serve as my Circuit's Special Victims Prosecutor. And over the course of the next decade, I would try more than thirty such cases to a jury – a few of which I will describe below.

The Alan Walker Case

When a four-year-old girl in Sarasota, Florida disclosed to a family friend in 1992 that her father had molested her at her grandparents' house in Newton County, Georgia, she was taken to a Child Advocacy Center where her detailed account of the abuse was videotaped by a trained forensic child interviewer. After a medical examination produced corroborating physical evidence,[55] Florida Department of Law Enforcement agents reported the allegations to Agent Troy Pierce of

---

by engaging in bad habits (drugs, alcohol, gambling, etc.) or associating with bad people (drug dealers, gang members, etc.).

[54] This is significant because Huggins was eligible to apply for parole after serving just seven years of his life sentence.

[55] Finding corroborating physical or medical evidence in a child molestation case is extremely rare – found in less than 5% of such cases. There are two reasons for this. One, child molesters typically "groom" their victims gradually and rarely need to exert physical force to obtain their victims' compliance. Two, child abuse victims rarely make contemporaneous reports of their abuse – their outcries often coming weeks or months and sometimes years later, thus giving their bodies time to heal. See https://www.ncjrs.gov/pdffiles1/nij/grants/252768.pdf

Georgia Bureau of Investigation (GBI). When Agent Pierce contacted me and related these facts, I agreed to prosecute the case and directed him to secure an arrest warrant for the suspect.

The suspect, Alan Walker, was a prison correctional officer who lived in Wilkinson County. But when police arrived at his trailer home to serve the arrest warrant, Walker was nowhere to be found. Instead, all they found was a puddle of blood on the bathroom floor and bullet holes in the ceiling tiles. It appeared at first glance that Walker had been shot and his body removed and disposed of. But appearances can be deceiving.

When GBI crime scene technicians arrived at the scene, they quickly concluded that the apparent crime scene had been "staged." In other words, this was not a crime scene at all; it was a *fake* crime scene. Although the blood appeared to be real, the blood patterns observed were inconsistent with patterns typically associated with gunshot wounds. And if Walker had in fact been shot, why would someone bother to remove and conceal his body? Agent Pierce theorized that Walker had gotten wind of his impending arrest and had attempted to fake his death to throw police off his trail. Agent Pierce's theory would ultimately be validated, but not until seven years later.

Walker's body eventually turned up. And he was very much alive. Paralleling the bizarre nature of his disappearance, he was found in a most unlikely place. When Walker attempted to purchase a firearm in Homer, Alaska – you read that right, I said Homer, *Alaska* – he foolishly attempted to do so in his *own* name. And when a routine background check[56] revealed that Walker still had an outstanding warrant

---

[56] Such background checks have been required since 1993 under the Brady Law named after President Reagan's Press Secretary Jim Brady. Brady was shot and seriously injured during an assassination attempt on Reagan's life in 1981.

in the state of Georgia, Walker was arrested by Alaska authorities and subsequently extradited to Georgia to stand trial.

But there was a "slight" complication. Walker's daughter, who was by then 11 years old, not only had no memory of her father's abuse, she had no memory of her father at all! This was, to say the least, a prosecutorial conundrum: How was I supposed to prove that Walker had molested his daughter if she couldn't even pick him out of a lineup? Fortunately, Georgia's child-friendly rules of evidence provided me with two viable weapons: One, Georgia's Child Hearsay Statute would permit me to introduce into evidence and play for the jury the child victim's videotaped forensic interview made seven years earlier. Two, Georgia law would allow me to argue that the timing and strange circumstances surrounding Walker's disappearance – so-called "flight" to avoid prosecution – was evidence of his consciousness of guilt with respect to his daughter's accusations. I concluded that these two critical pieces of evidence – combined with the testimony of the Sarasota physician who had examined the child and found injuries consistent with sexual abuse – would likely be enough to secure a conviction.

To prepare for trial, my investigator Joe Rickman and I flew to Tampa and drove to Sarasota to meet and interview our witnesses. All told, we met with ten witnesses before returning to Georgia the following day. It was a whirlwind trip. But the police investigators and Child Advocacy Center personnel could not have been more cooperative. Even the examining physician was on board. At considerable expense, we flew all of these Florida witnesses to Georgia to testify at Walker's trial. And despite contentious jury deliberations that pitted one holdout juror against the other eleven, Walker was eventually convicted – albeit of only one of the ten counts alleged in the indictment.

Contentious jury deliberations? Allow me to explain. Trial judges typically instruct trial jurors before the trial begins that they are prohibited from doing *any* investigation on their own – that they must base their verdict *solely* on the evidence presented in the courtroom. Moreover, jurors are instructed not to be concerned with punishment, but to focus solely on the guilt or innocence of the accused. Most jurors obey their oaths as jurors and comply with these instructions, but one juror in the Walker case did not.

After a long day of jury deliberations, the jury appeared to be at an impasse. It appeared that we were heading for a hung jury and a mistrial. The judge, however, sent the jury home for the night and brought them back the next morning to continue their deliberations. Within minutes, a female juror emerged from the jury room crying hysterically and insisted that the judge allow her to speak with him. When the judge, the defense attorney, and I met with this juror in the judge's chambers, she advised us that the other jurors were being "mean" to her. To address this juror's concerns, the judge brought the entire jury back into the courtroom, cautioned them that they should consider the opinions of all of their fellow jurors in arriving at their verdict, and sent them back to the jury room to continue their deliberations.

Not long after deliberations resumed, the jury alerted the court that it had reached a verdict. When the verdict form was read, however, the jury had only returned a guilty verdict on one count of the 10-count indictment. With respect to the other nine counts, the jury announced that it could not reach a unanimous verdict. The judge thereafter accepted their guilty verdict, declared mistrials as to the other nine counts, dismissed the jury, and sentenced Walker to ten years in prison.[57]

---

[57] Upon Walker's agreement not to appeal his lone conviction, I agreed not to retry the nine mistried counts.

After the jury had been released, I learned that the "hysterical juror" was the only juror who had opposed convicting Walker on all 10 counts. Her reason? She had done internet research *during* the trial about the sentence that could be imposed for the crime of child molestation – in clear violation of the judge's instruction *not* to do any independent research. And when she learned that the indictment against Walker carried a *potential* sentence of 200 years in prison (20 years on each of the 10 counts), she decided that she couldn't vote to convict – in clear violation of the judge's instruction *not* to be concerned with punishment.

In the end, this juror finally capitulated and agreed to vote guilty on one count. Had we known before the verdict was announced that this juror had violated the judge's instructions, however, we could have replaced her with an alternate juror, and we likely would have secured ten convictions instead of one.

Thus, like the "staged" shooting incident in his trailer home seven years earlier, Walker had once again "dodged a bullet" – this time, however, it was a figurative one.

The William Walsh "Schoolteacher" Case[58]

In 1996, the Social Circle School System in Walton County hired a 49-year-old man named William Walsh to teach its Gifted Program. In this position, Walsh would be responsible for supplementing the education of "gifted" students in grades 1 through 5, i.e., the "smart kids." These children would visit Walsh's classroom several times a week to engage in special activities like building Lego structures and playing

---

[58] Walsh v. State, 236 Ga. App. 558 (1999) (Oconee County case); Walsh v. State, 302 Ga. App. 461 (2010) (Walton County case).

board games. Walsh's students came to love these non-traditional class-room activities – and Mr. Walsh.

Within six weeks from the beginning of the school year, however, nine boys ranging in age from 7 to 10 came forward to accuse Walsh of inappropriate touching. When confronted with these allegations, Walsh admitted to being an affectionate teacher, but denied touching any of these children inappropriately. But rather than fighting to save his job and reputation, Walsh offered to resign - an offer that school administrators hurriedly accepted. Walsh apparently hoped that his speedy resignation would result in the matter being dropped. But school administrators – as required by Georgia's Mandated Reporter Law – reported these disturbing allegations to authorities and a joint Department of Family & Children Services (DFCS) / law enforcement investigation ensued.

When questioned by investigators, 8 of the 9 boys at the Social Circle school reported non-genital touching of their butts, backs, or stomachs. Some of these boys alleged that Walsh had only touched them over their clothes, but others alleged that Walsh had used his hands or fingers to explore beneath their clothing and touched their bare skin. The ninth boy, however, alleged that Walsh had made direct contact with his genitalia – albeit over his clothing. Upon examining each of the children's statements, my initial task was to determine: Was this particular child describing an offense of child molestation as defined by Georgia law? And if so, how was I going to prove it?

In Georgia, the crime of Child Molestation is defined as occurring when a person performs an "immoral or indecent act" to, with, or in the presence of a child under the age of 16 with the "intent to arouse or satisfy his sexual desires." I was confident that the ninth boy's allegation of over-the-clothes genital touching would meet this definition.

But would the allegations of non-genital touching made by the other eight boys also qualify? I concluded that they would.

First, I knew that Georgia law would permit the trial jury to decide for themselves if – in light of local community standards – Walsh's acts were "immoral or indecent." And in making this determination, the jury would be permitted to consider the totality of the circumstances surrounding the alleged acts. Second, based upon the fact that not one, not two, but nine boys were making similar allegations – I believed that I could convince the jury that Walsh's acts had been committed with requisite criminal intent, i.e., to satisfy his sexual desires. So, I proceeded to indict Walsh on nine counts of child molestation.[59]

Convincing myself, however, was not the same thing as convincing a jury. I knew that it was going to be a challenge to prove that Walsh had touched these children – not just inadvertently, accidentally, or affectionately – but for his own sexual gratification. And I knew that some jurors would be naturally skeptical of accusations made by a child against an adult and would be inclined to give the adult the benefit of the doubt. I needed something to convince the jury that all of these touches were connected, a part of a greater pattern of sexual abuse. Fortunately, investigators provided me with two damning pieces of corroborative evidence – both of which I was able to use at Walsh's trial.

One, during their investigation, investigators were shocked to learn that this was not the first time that Walsh had been accused of inappropriately touching school children. In fact, he had been accused

---

[59] When the parents of one of the boys insisted that their child not be forced to testify, I reluctantly agreed not to pursue that count of the indictment.

of inappropriately touching school children on *two* previous occasions! In the first case, a Gilmer County grand jury had no billed charges accusing Walsh of molesting twin 8-year-old boys at the school where Walsh taught.[60] In the second case, two pre-adolescent boys at an Oconee County middle school where Walsh was substitute teaching accused Walsh of touching them on their buttocks. And a third boy accused Walsh of touching his privates. The latter allegation was witnessed by a female classmate. Inexplicably, however, school administrators failed to report these allegations to the proper authorities.[61]

Two, during their investigation, investigators discovered that Walsh had been a photojournalist prior to becoming a schoolteacher. And in their interviews with teachers at Walsh's school, investigators learned that Walsh had been seen taking numerous photographs of kids at school – in his classroom and on the playground. With this information in hand, we sought a search warrant for Walsh's home computer to see if he had taken any *inappropriate* photographs of these children.[62] After making a forensic copy of the hard drive from Walsh's computer, a computer analyst from the GBI discovered reams of sexually suggestive photographs of adolescent boys. None, however, were of

---

[60] I later learned from the District Attorney in Gilmer County that there had been five school teachers on that Gilmer County grand jury and that they had expressed concerns about (and were hypersensitive to) the possibility of false accusations against school teachers.

[61] Rather than notify DFCS or police, school administrators simply chose to remove Walsh's name from the roster of approved substitute teachers. The administrators' actions arguably violated Georgia's Mandated Reporter Law, but years later an Oconee County grand jury would decline to indict them.

[62] We were able to get a search warrant for Walsh's computer in part because we persuaded the issuing magistrate that child molesters frequently keep "trophies" – including photographs – by which to remember their victims. And lo and behold, guess what investigators found during the search of Walsh's home? They found a photograph of the twin boys Walsh had allegedly molested in Gilmer County years earlier!

my child victims or any other Social Circle student. Nonetheless, after convincing the trial judge that these photographs were relevant to show Walsh's sexual interest in young boys, I was permitted to show enlarged images of these photographs to a visibly shocked jury at Walsh's trial.

Perhaps equally damaging to Walsh's defense was his decision to waive his 5th Amendment privilege and testify. Like many of the child molesters that I had encountered, Walsh believed that he was too smart to get caught, and if caught, he was clever enough to talk his way out of trouble. On the stand, Walsh was smug and arrogant. These children and their teachers, he claimed, had conspired to falsely accuse him. Specifically, he claimed that the teachers were jealous of his popularity with the students and resentful of his views on Evolution. And he claimed that many of the alleged victims belonged to the same church youth group where they were able to conspire with one another and devise a secret plot against him. The thrust of his defense? He was simply an affectionate teacher and the victim of a witch hunt.

What followed was my only "Perry Mason" moment in court. On cross-examination I referenced the images from his computer that I had shown to the jury, and fully expecting a vociferous denial, I asked Mr. Walsh:

> "You found these images of half-dressed adolescent boys sexually arousing, didn't you!?"

And to a stunned courtroom, Walsh replied, "Some of it." If any member of the jury was still harboring lingering doubts about Walsh's deviant sexual interest in children, surely, at that point, such doubts had been erased.

The jury thereafter returned guilty verdicts on four of the eight counts, an acquittal on one count, and was equally divided on the remaining three counts. Although a guilty verdict on all counts would have been nice, it was unnecessary. The jury had given us convictions on four felonies – each carrying a potential sentence of 20 years in prison. Following a pre-sentence investigation, Walsh was sentenced to 40 years in prison.

* * *

Walsh was later prosecuted and convicted of molesting the three boys in Oconee County as well and received an additional 20 years confinement. His appeal of that conviction was denied, but curiously, he did not pursue a timely appeal of his Walton County convictions. Years later, however, he was granted an out-of-time appeal of his Walton County convictions due to his attorney's negligence. Having been in prison for years at that point, he was eligible for court-appointed counsel to assist him with his appeal. Despite the fact that I was teaching at UGA Law at the time, I volunteered to write the State's appellate brief. Like his first appeal, that appeal was also denied.[63]

* * *

Please permit me to share with you a humorous aside here. Crime is serious business. But prosecutors sometimes see the humor in otherwise troubling circumstances. Perhaps it's a defense mechanism – something that allows us to cope with the dark side of humanity. So here it is:

---

[63] Walsh thereafter pursued a writ of certiorari to the Georgia Supreme Court. That being a so-called "discretionary appeal," he was no longer entitled to court-appointed counsel, so he represented himself. Now pro se, he drafted a rambling 150-page, handwritten brief. The Georgia Supreme Court later dismissed it in a two-sentence order.

After Walsh's conviction, he was housed in the Athens-Clarke County jail while awaiting transfer to the state prison system. While there, he attempted to intervene in a dispute between two county detainees – one of whom had recently been convicted of capital murder and sentenced to death. Bad move. When Walsh attempted to separate the two combatants, the murderer (á la boxer Mike Tyson) bit off a chunk of Walsh's ear!

The William Posey Case

See CHAPTER 11 – Crimes of Unspeakable Evil, The William Posey Case.

All told, I tried 34 child molestation cases in my prosecution career. Twenty-eight of these defendants were convicted, two were acquitted, and four trials ended in a mistrial. And I prosecuted many other defendants charged with child molestation who pled guilty without the necessity of a trial. Of all of my accomplishments as a prosecutor and District Attorney, I am most proud of my prioritization of these cases and my role in bringing justice to these children and their families.

CHAPTER 3

Murder & Manslaughter

When the general public thinks about crime, they usually think about violent crimes – especially murder and manslaughter. Both of these crimes fall under the general legal definition of "homicide" – the death of one human at the hands of another. I suppose that we shouldn't be surprised by this. After all, if one tunes in to watch their local TV news at six o'clock, he or she is likely going to hear about the latest homicide – often in gory, graphic detail. As they say in the broadcast news business, "If it bleeds, it leads."

I tried 21 homicide cases in my prosecution career. Of these, 17 resulted in convictions, 3 resulted in acquittals, and one ended in a mistrial (that I later successfully retried.) The stakes in these high-profile cases were extremely high. And I owed it to the families of these victims and to the community at large to give it my all. Fortunately, I had a lot of help. First of all, I had an outstanding staff of investigators, administrative assistants, secretaries, and victim advocates.[64] Second, I was privileged to work with many dedicated and talented law enforcement officers[65] who worked tirelessly to gather evidence in these cases

---

[64] See Chapter 15 – A Team Approach.

[65] A few of my favorites were Ray Parker, Travis Brown, Mike McHugh, Barney Manders, Lamar Palmer, Al Yarbrough, Drexell Booker, Chris Cannon, Glenn Yancey, Ronnie Sorrells, Tom

and many skilled criminalists[66] at the GBI Crime Lab who helped connect the dots.

In order to fully appreciate the distinction between murder and manslaughter and what it takes to secure a conviction for each offense, perhaps a brief definition of these terms is in order.

In Georgia, the crime of murder comes in two varieties: malice murder and felony murder. (Georgia doesn't recognize murder in the first degree, second degree, etc.) Georgia defines a malice murder as occurring when a person "unlawfully and with malice aforethought ... causes the death of another human being." Malice is defined as the "deliberate intention unlawfully to take the life of another human being" and may be "implied where no considerable provocation appears and where all the circumstances of the killing show an abandoned and malignant heart." No particular amount of premeditation is required to prove malice murder. Felony murder, on the other hand, occurs when a person causes the death of another human being *irrespective* of malice while in the commission of a felony, e.g., during an armed robbery. A conviction for either malice murder or felony murder authorizes a potential penalty of death, life without parole, or life imprisonment with the possibility of parole.[67]

Wilcox, and Greg Adcock (WCSO); Dell Reed, Charles Roper, Marty Roberts, Gwen Hightower, Keith Crum, Doug Kitchens, Mike Smith, Robbie Ballard, Jimmy Byrd, and Charles Ammons (NCSO); Almond Turner, Craig Treadwell, Rick Miller, Ken Malcom, Philip Bradford, Arvo Bowen, and Wendell Wagstaff (CPD); Mike Burke, David Hannah, and Emily Mapp (MPD); Mike Pearson, Troy Pierce, Marty Zon, Fred Mays, Bobby Stanley, Dow Nicholson, and Ben Williams (GBI); Mike Welch and Cliff Miller (GSP). My apologies to the many others not mentioned here.

[66] My favorites included: Sam House (crime scene analysis), Kelly Fite (ballistics), Lou Cuendet (fingerprints), Dr. Mark Koponen (autopsies), Gretchen Hancock (drug identification), and Janet Honeycutt (criminal profiling). My apologies to the many others not mentioned here.

[67] See O.C.G.A. 16-5-1.

The offense of voluntary manslaughter occurs when a person "causes the death of another human being under circumstances which would otherwise be murder and if he acts solely as the result of a sudden, violent, and irresistible passion resulting from serious provocation sufficient to excite such passion in a reasonable person." The maximum penalty for voluntary manslaughter is 20 years confinement.[68]

The cases described below are a few of my more memorable, non-death penalty murder and manslaughter trials. (I describe my death penalty cases in Chapter 10.)

The Jamie Martin Case[69]

I tried my first murder case in 1991 shortly after becoming District Attorney. The case involved a young man named Jamie Martin who was accused of murdering his mother – with two baseball bats and an iron pipe! According to the medical examiner, the victim was struck at least 5 times in the head. As you can imagine, it was a gruesome crime scene. To make matters worse – if that's even possible, the victim's body was not discovered until hours later when it was found in the trunk of her car.

When confronted by police, Martin initially blamed his mother's boyfriend for the crime. But as the evidence against him mounted, he shifted theories and at trial attempted to convince the jury that this was a crime of passion triggered by his mother's excessive drinking. In other words, if he was guilty of anything, it was voluntary manslaughter, not murder. But despite claiming that his mother had provoked his 3-tooled attack upon her, he maintained that he had no actual memory of killing her. To explain why, Martin presented the testimony of

[68] See O.C.G.A. 16-5-2.

[69] Martin v. State, 262 Ga. 312 (1992).

a psychologist who testified that Martin suffered "psychotic amnesia" following the crime.

Unfortunately for Martin, the State had already undermined his manslaughter/amnesia theory through the testimony of several witnesses during the State's case-in-chief. First of all, several witnesses testified that Martin had discussed killing his mother *weeks* before the crime. Second, a crime scene tech testified that there was evidence to suggest that on the morning after the killing, Martin had attempted to clean up the bloody crime scene to conceal his actions. And finally, Martin's girlfriend testified that Martin had purchased gasoline to burn his mother's body in the trunk of her car but apparently couldn't bring himself to light the match.

Thus, it was no surprise when the jury rejected Martin's manslaughter theory and found him guilty of malice murder. He was thereafter sentenced to life imprisonment.

* * *

Ironically, the defense attorney in the Martin case, Gene Benton, had been the Walton County assistant district attorney whose job I took years earlier when he left to enter private practice.[70] And paradoxically, I had unsuccessfully prosecuted Martin's mother for DUI just two years prior to her murder. A strange coincidence indeed.

* * *

I tried three murder cases in my first full year as District Attorney and three more the following year. (Well, I guess I asked for the job.) In fact, it seemed like murders in my Circuit increased precipitously upon

---

[70] Benton became a successful civil attorney and served as the City Attorney for the City of Monroe for many years prior to his election to the Alcovy Circuit Superior Court bench in 2004.

my election – a fact that did not go unnoticed by my staff. One day, as I entered my office in Walton County, I was greeted by a phony "chalk outline" of a dead body on the carpet in my office.

The Candace Valenti Case

I tried my best to persuade Candace Valenti and her attorney to accept my plea offer to serve a 5-year prison sentence for voluntary manslaughter. But she wouldn't budge. So, in early 1992, I had no choice but to try her.

Why such a "sweet" plea offer, you may ask? Well, as far as killers go, Valenti was a somewhat sympathetic one. For starters, she was just 20 years old. She lived with her mother and her mother's much, much younger boyfriend. According to Valenti, her mother and the boyfriend quarreled with one another on a regular basis. And on the day of the killing, her mother and the boyfriend were at it again. Valenti had had enough. She yelled at the boyfriend to stop – "or else." The boyfriend just laughed and asked her what she was going to do about it. To which Valenti, responded, "I'll kill you." The boyfriend then calmly strode to a back bedroom with Valenti quick on his heels. He grabbed a revolver, handed it to her, and dared her to shoot him. Unflinchingly, Valenti placed the revolver against the boyfriend's forehead and squeezed the trigger. The gun was loaded. The boyfriend was dead.

Without a doubt, this deceased young man's actions contributed to his own death. But legally speaking, Valenti had not been justified in using deadly force that day to rid herself (and her mother) of the boyfriend's boorish behavior. Valenti could have called 911 or she could have called a cab, but she couldn't do what she did. In my mind, it was a clear-cut case of voluntary manslaughter. Valenti had acted, not with malice aforethought, but as the result of "a sudden, violent, and irresistible passion resulting from serious provocation sufficient to excite such passion in a reasonable person."

When Newton County Investigator Charles Roper interrogated Valenti following her arrest, he asked her to show him how the shooting had occurred. In a very forthcoming, and highly incriminating way, Valenti obliged by pressing her index finger – representing the barrel of the gun – against Roper's forehead. To re-enact this jailhouse confession during the trial, I asked Investigator Roper to step off the witness stand, hold the actual murder weapon, and show the jury what Valenti had shown him – with me playing the role of the victim. So, yes, those assembled in the courtroom that day witnessed the barrel of a real revolver being pressed against the forehead of their District Attorney. Of course, the gun was unloaded. But still, in hindsight, not one of my brighter ideas.

I'll never know if my courtroom theatrics contributed to the outcome, but Valenti was convicted of voluntary manslaughter and Judge Ott sentenced her to the maximum penalty of 20 years in prison.[71] Although I was satisfied that the verdict was just, I didn't agree with the severity of the judge's sentence. I couldn't help but think that Valenti was a victim as well as a killer. So, when Valenti asked the state's Sentence Review Panel to modify her sentence, I took the highly unusual step of writing a letter to the Panel asking that it reduce her sentence. And in an extraordinarily rare reversal of a Georgia trial judge's sentencing discretion, the Panel later cut Valenti's sentence in half![72]

---

[71] It did not help Valenti's cause that she gave three different accounts of the shooting. She told police that she had acted in anger. She told her attorney that she had acted in self-defense. And then she told the jury that it was an accident.

[72] Valenti never pursued her other appellate remedies.

The Gaynor Bracewell, Jr. Case[73]

On the western edge of Walton County, there is a community known as High Shoals. For years, this community was dominated by the Bracewell family. The patriarch of the family, Gaynor Bracewell, Sr., ran the hydroelectric plant on the Apalachee River that ran through the middle of High Shoals and was the dividing line between Walton and Oconee Counties.[74]

By the late 1990s, Gaynor's son, Gaynor, Jr., lived in a modest, colonial-style house on the Walton County side of the river. Gaynor, Jr.'s troubles began in this case when he met and started dating an older divorcee with two sons. It was a tumultuous relationship. Gaynor and the woman would frequently drink to excess – and fight loudly with one another. After several breakups, however, the divorcee and her sons moved into his house. This arrangement would prove to be Gaynor, Jr.'s undoing.

While living under the same roof and unbeknownst to the boys' mother, the older boy, aged 17, hereinafter "the boy," and Gaynor, Jr. allegedly did drugs together. Before long, the boy was caught with marijuana that he had allegedly obtained from Gaynor, Jr., and the boy was placed on juvenile probation. When his mother learned about the alleged source of her son's weed, she threatened once again to end her relationship with Gaynor, Jr.

Late one evening, the divorcee sat in her car in Gaynor, Jr.'s driveway and began working her way through the 12-pack of beer that she had just purchased. When Gaynor, Jr. came outside to try to sweet-talk her inside, all hell broke loose. The cussing and screaming could

---

[73] Bracewell v. State, 243 Ga. App. 792 (2000).

[74] High Shoals is just south of the Moore's Ford Bridge area described in Chapter 6 – Whodunit Cases, The Moore's Ford "Mass Lynching" Case.

probably have been heard on the other side of the Apalachee River. At one point, the woman began chasing Gaynor, Jr. throughout the house – even kicking in a locked door behind which Gaynor, Jr. had sought refuge. But eventually, the two took their brouhaha out to the front porch directly underneath the boy's bedroom window on the second floor.

The boy, who had endured many such episodes in the past, had had enough. He grabbed his pistol (which a person of his young age, not to mention one on juvenile probation, had no business possessing) and ran downstairs to the front porch to confront Gaynor, Jr. When the boy emerged through the front door onto the porch with gun in hand, Gaynor, Jr. immediately darted for the front door. After Gaynor, Jr. was safely inside the house, the boy took a stance in the front yard and exclaimed, "I'm tired of this s---!" He then fired the pistol once into the air and once into the yard.

Hearing these gunshots, Gaynor, Jr. ran to his bedroom, loaded his 12-gauge shotgun, and took a defensive position in the kitchen with an unobstructed view of the front door. According to the boy's mother, several minutes passed and the situation outside began to calm down. She claimed that her son threw the gun down in the yard before attempting to re-enter the house. And before he opened the door, he said, "Gaynor, I don't have my gun, I'm coming in." But as soon as the boy opened the door and took one step across the threshold, a shotgun blast rang out. The boy was struck in his midsection and bled out before the arrival of the ambulance. And by the time police arrived, Gaynor, Jr. had run out the back door into the darkness and was nowhere to be found.[75]

---

[75] One of my main concerns about this case was the fact that I had to rely primarily on the mother's testimony regarding the sequence of events. One, I knew that she had consumed several

When I reviewed the evidence, it appeared to me that Gaynor, Jr. had decided to shoot the boy as soon as he opened the door – whether the boy was armed or unarmed. Thus, in my mind, it was not a legitimate case of self-defense. On the other hand, given the threatening encounter that had occurred just prior to the shooting, I felt that Gaynor, Jr.'s actions were more likely the result of passion than clear-headed deliberation. Thus, I decided to seek an indictment for voluntary manslaughter instead of murder. That decision did not please the boy's mother or the other members of her family – especially the boy's grandmother.

Before the next scheduled grand jury session, the dead boy's grandmother contacted several grand jurors in an attempt to influence their decision. Although the grand jury ultimately agreed with me and indicted Gaynor, Jr. on manslaughter charges, I was livid when I heard what the grandmother had done. So much so that I called her into my office and threatened to charge her with tampering with a grand jury – a felony offense. Needless to say, my relationship with the victim's family was rather strained thereafter.

Sgt. Ray Parker with the Walton County Sherriff's Office investigated this case. Sgt. Parker was one of my all-time favorite investigators. He was a very dogged, thorough investigator – and funny as hell. He had a very cynical view of human nature that struck me as hilarious – and was, for the most part, right on the money. And his assessment of this case was no exception. He took an immediate dislike to Gaynor, Jr., who had displayed a very pusillanimous, whiny attitude about the whole affair – one consistent with his actions on the night of the shooting.

---

beers prior to the shooting incident. Two, she clearly had no love for Gaynor, Jr. at this point. Fortunately, her younger son was also present that night and corroborated much of her testimony.

What I think ultimately cinched the case was Sgt. Parker's decision to re-enact the shooting on videotape. The camera was set up in the kitchen – which would have been Gaynor, Jr.'s point of view as the victim attempted to re-enter the house through the front door. With the camera rolling, Parker entered the front door to show how the boy would have appeared to Gaynor, Jr. – with the left side of his body visible first. This was consistent with the autopsy report that described the shotgun pellets entering the *left side* of the boy's body and traveling from left to right as they traversed his abdomen. This was also consistent with our theory that the boy had been shot as soon as he set foot inside the doorway.

Most criminal defense attorneys advise their clients not to take the stand, i.e., to invoke their 5th Amendment privilege against self-incrimination and refuse to testify. The reason? More often than not, a defendant's testimony falls apart on the stand when subjected to the crucible of cross-examination. Fortunately for us, Gaynor, Jr. ignored this sage advice and elected to testify on his own behalf. In an apparent attempt to bolster his self-defense claim, Gaynor, Jr. claimed that the boy had gotten *all the way* into the house and had taken a defensive position, albeit armed, behind the fireplace mantle. Then, Gaynor, Jr. claimed that the victim jumped out with the gun in his right hand, right arm outstretched, and pointed the gun at him menacingly. If true, that would have put the *right side* of the boy's body facing Gaynor, Jr. at the time the shotgun was fired. But that scenario was totally inconsistent with the autopsy report. According to the autopsy, the path of the shotgun pellets was left to right, not right to left! Gaynor, Jr. was lying.

To lock Gaynor, Jr. into his testimony on direct, I asked him on cross-examination to step down from the witness stand and show the jury exactly how the boy was standing when he was shot. He foolishly did so and doubled-down on his testimony on direct. This deprived his attorney of any wiggle room on re-direct examination. Taking the stand was a big mistake. His untenable theory was now set in cement.

The jury convicted Gaynor, Jr. of voluntary manslaughter, and he was sentenced to 20 years in prison. The boy's family continued to claim, however, that Gaynor, Jr. had gotten away with murder. For my part, however, I was relieved. Given the dubious credibility of my non-law enforcement witnesses, the jury easily could have acquitted him outright. I suppose this illustrates the fact that prosecution is rarely a zero-sum game in which there is a clear winner and a clear loser. As a prosecutor, you quickly learn that the pursuit of justice often results in *neither* side being completely happy with the end result.[76]

The James Brown "Taxi Cab Murder" Case[77]

On the list of the most dangerous jobs in America, driving a taxicab probably ranks near the top. Think about it. Cab drivers pick up total strangers at sometimes unfamiliar locations en route to equally unfamiliar destinations – all with their backs turned on the customer. Sadly, in the case that follows, that proposition hit close to home.

One afternoon in 1997, taxi driver Vickie Forrester was dispatched to pick up a fare at Newton General Hospital. Upon her arrival at the pick-up location, she met a young, skinny kid named James Brown.[78] Brown directed her to drop him off on a rural dirt road outside the city limits of Covington. But rather than paying the cab fare, he got out and stood at the front passenger door, aimed a .22 pistol at her head and neck, and fired twice. Next, he proceeded to pull

---

[76] Bracewell's conviction was later reversed due to a jury instruction error. But rather than face the prospect of a retrial, he pled guilty and received a reduced sentence.

[77] Brown v State, 274 Ga. 202 (2001).

[78] No relation to the Godfather of Soul, James Brown, who famously sang Dooley's Junkyard Dogs at Georgia Bulldog games when I was in college at UGA.

Forrester's body from the taxi onto the dirt road. Then, he removed the "Taxi" insignia from the car doors, stepped over Forrester's body, and climbed into the driver's seat. As he drove off, he ran over Forrester's body leaving a zigzag tire print on her right leg.

When Forrester failed to respond to the taxi company dispatcher's repeated calls, the owner of the company became worried and went to look for her. But a landscaper working in the area where her body had been dumped spotted her first and notified police. Soon thereafter, police arrived to discover Forrester's lifeless, twisted body lying in the roadway. A statewide search for the taxicab ensued. Within hours, Henry County police located it in the parking lot of the Patrick Henry Alternative School in Henry County about an hour south of Covington.[79] Brown and the pistol he had used to kill Forrester were both still in the car. And despite having just committed a brutal homicide hours earlier, Brown was found taking a nap on the front seat at the time of his arrest.

It was an incomprehensibly senseless crime. Was this a robbery? A motor vehicle theft? A thrill killing? No, as it turns out, Brown simply needed transportation so he could go see a student at the Henry County school – a girl with whom he had been carrying on a long-distance relationship. Apparently, Brown's mother had refused to let him borrow her car, and he simply wanted to see this girl in the worst way – literally, in the worst way.

After reviewing Brown's case file, I was still having difficulty wrapping my head around the motive in this case. Could Brown really have killed Forrester simply to gain access to a car? On the eve of the trial, I learned the answer. To prepare for trial, I had driven to Henry

---

[79] This school was later used as a film set in the Netflix series Stanger Things where Will, Mike, Lucas, and Dustin battle the "Upside Down's" Demogorgan.

County to meet with Brown's "telephone girlfriend" Nicole. In the living room of her home, I learned for the first time that Brown had called Nicole from jail following his arrest – apparently using his proverbial "one phone call." She told me that during this phone call, Brown confessed to her that he had shot and killed a taxi cab driver "for her" so they could be together.

Brown, who was just 16 years of age, was tried as an adult. Due to Brown's youth, however, the death penalty was not an option.[80] At trial, Brown claimed that he had acted in self-defense. He had told investigators following his arrest that Forrester pulled a gun on him and that he had been forced to "smoke her." The jury didn't buy it. Brown was convicted and sentenced to life imprisonment.

Thus, ironically, in a case that had invoked the name of Virginia Statesman Patrick Henry, who famously said "Give me liberty, or give me death!," the Georgia criminal justice system gave Brown neither.

The David Scott George "No Body" Case

In criminal cases, the prosecution must ordinarily prove the *corpus delicti*, i.e., the "body of the crime." In a murder case, for example, the prosecution must prove that a murder has actually taken place – something that *ordinarily* requires the prosecution to produce the body of the murder victim. Thus, if the deceased's body is not found, a defendant may not ordinarily be convicted of that person's murder – even if he has confessed to killing that person.

But he confessed, you say! True, but not all confessions are reliable. Verifiable cases of suspects confessing to crimes that they didn't

---

[80] At the time of Brown's crime, Georgia law prohibited the imposition of the death penalty against a person who was under the age of 17 at the time of the crime. The United States Supreme Court would later hold in Roper v. Simmons (2005) that the 8th Amendment prohibits the execution of a person for a crime committed before his 18th birthday.

commit are well-documented. These so-called "false confessions" some-times occur when a suspect is pressured into giving a statement by an overbearing police investigator. And then, there's the rare suspect who falsely confesses to achieve some degree of fame or notoriety.[81] One way to guard against such false confessions is to require the prosecution to at least show that the confessed-to crime actually occurred. Hence, the *corpus delicti* rule.

You probably noticed that I said that the prosecution in a mur-der case must "ordinarily" produce the body of the murder victim. The word "ordinarily" is a term that is all-too-familiar to law students, for as you quickly learn in law school, there's almost always an exception to every rule.[82] The exception to the corpus delicti rule, however, is a very narrow one. Consequently, by the 1990s, there had only been a handful of successful "no body" murder prosecutions in the United States. In those cases, the prosecution was able to present substan-tial circumstantial evidence that the victim, though still missing, was almost certainly dead. In the David Scott George case described below, I was forced to rely on this rare, narrow exception.

There was strong reason to believe that David Scott George had killed his estranged girlfriend and mother of his 5-year-old son. George's ex-girlfriend, Allison Rambeau, routinely left her small chil-dren with her mother while she worked. But one day, inexplicably, she failed to pick them up at the end of her shift. This had never happened before. And when her family went to look for Allison at her home, she

---

[81] The JonBenet Ramsey case illustrates this point. In that case, a man named John Mark Karr allegedly confessed to killing JonBenet, a Colorado child, and was extradited to the United States from Thailand. But it was later determined that Karr's DNA didn't match samples from the crime scene and he was apparently in Alabama with his wife at the time JonBenet was killed!

[82] As I would often tell my law students, "Law is all about 'wavy lines' and 'gray areas.' If you want certainty, you should pursue a career in the hard sciences like mathematics where $2 + 2$ will always equal 4."

wasn't there. Police were notified and joined the search. But her body was nowhere to be found. Foul play was suspected. So naturally, the first person police questioned was David George.

After repeated denials, George finally confessed that he had in fact killed Allison. He claimed that he and Allison had argued at her house and that the argument grew violent. After choking her to the point of unconsciousness, he said that he carried her limp body to the bathroom, filled the bathtub with water, and drowned her. He then wrapped her body in a garbage bag and a white sheet and placed it in the trunk of his car. Later that night, under the cover of darkness, he placed Allison's body in a commercial trash bin adjacent to a restaurant on Highway 138 in nearby Rockdale County.

George's detailed confession had the ring of truth. Thus, investigators rushed to the restaurant named by George only to discover that the trash bin had already been emptied – over a week earlier. Next step: Where had the trash been taken? Investigators learned that the restaurant's trash was emptied at the Jackson County landfill. Next step: Could the body be located in the landfill? The lead investigator Doug Kitchens and I traveled to the landfill and asked the owner where we should start looking. The answer we received was devastating. Because Allison's body had been deposited in the landfill over a week earlier, we were told that it was likely located at least 30 feet below the surface *somewhere* on the landfill's 8-acre tract of land.

30 feet below? 8 acres? Even assuming that George had told us the truth about where he had dumped Allison's body, the odds of finding her body in the landfill were no better than finding the proverbial needle in a haystack.[83] But if we didn't produce Allison's body,

---

[83] There were two additional complicating factors: (1) We were quoted a $1 million price tag for a grid search of the landfill, and (2) we were told that we couldn't use cadaver dogs to assist in

could we prove the *corpus delicti*? After exploring all other options, I made the decision to pursue murder charges against George without Allison's body.

By the time the trial date arrived in early 1999, I had extensively researched the history of "no body" prosecutions and prepared a detailed trial brief – outlining the legal history of the *corpus delicti* rule and the handful of cases that had satisfied the exception to the rule. The common denominator in these cases was the presence of large quantities of the victim's blood at the crime scene combined with expert medical testimony that the victim could not have survived that degree of blood loss.[84] But I didn't have that in the George case – she had allegedly been drowned. I was forced to rely instead on a combination of factors including the acrimonious history between George and the deceased, the fact that she had never abandoned her young children before, and the fact that her credit cards and bank account had had no activity since the date of her disappearance. My argument: Given these facts, Allison must surely be dead.

In Georgia, as in most jurisdictions, a defendant may make a mid-trial motion for a "directed verdict of acquittal" after the prosecution has rested its case-in-chief. If the judge is convinced that the prosecution has failed to carry its burden of proof – including the *corpus delicti*, he or she can take the case from the jury and acquit the defendant. Going into this case, I knew that the judge's ruling on George's directed verdict motion was going to be a close call. I had my trial brief ready.

---

the search because there were too many competing scents in the landfill – and it would "ruin" the dogs.

[84] The most prominent of these cases was a California case involving one of the Manson Family killings. See People v. Manson, 71 Cal.App.3d 1 (1977).

But I will never know if my proposed exception to the *corpus delicti* rule would have prevailed in the George case. To everyone's surprise, George decided to plead guilty during the trial after he heard his taped confession played for the jury. To this day, a small part of me still wishes that this case had sidestepped a directed verdict of acquittal and proceeded to a jury verdict of guilty. Had that occurred, the Georgia Supreme Court would have been asked to rule upon the validity of my *corpus delicti* exception theory. I must acknowledge, however, that securing George's life sentence for the murder of his ex-girlfriend was far more important than satisfying my academic curiosity.

The Richard Walker "Farmhouse Execution" Case

Two men were bound with duct tape and electrical cords, blindfolded, and shot in the back of the head execution-style at a farmhouse in rural Newton County. Miraculously, one lived. The two men were allegedly homosexual lovers. And the dead man was reportedly a methamphetamine dealer. Both of these factors would complicate this rural Georgia prosecution in the early 1990s.[85] To further complicate matters, the crime scene was a bloody mess and responding officers – fearing the risk of HIV/AIDS – failed to adequately document the crime scene and preserve evidence.

The surviving victim, to say the least, was a very shaky witness. The victim told police that two men had come to the victims' farmhouse that night to rob them, but denied that the robbery was drug-related. After speaking with others familiar with the farm, however, it became abundantly clear to me that the robbers came to the farm that

---

[85] Don't misinterpret this observation. I believe that one's sexual orientation is genetically predetermined. So, I did not attach any moral significance to these men's relationship, but I did to their alleged drug-dealing. More to the point, I feared that my rural Newton County jury pool would likely have misgivings about both

night looking for drugs and drug money. Although police later identified Richard Walker as one of the two alleged robbers, the identity of the second robber was never established.[86]

The evidence in this murder case was underwhelming at best. Nonetheless, after reviewing the evidence, I was firmly convinced of Walker's guilt. If I hadn't been, I wouldn't have tried the case.[87] But I knew that this prosecution was going to be an uphill battle.[88] My fears were later realized when the State's case utterly fell apart at the trial in late 1992. Walker's defense attorney, John Howell, absolutely destroyed the surviving victim on cross-examination.[89] And he deftly highlighted all of the investigation's miscues.

As the trial progressed, I began to question my involvement in this prosecution. I still believed that Walker had committed the crime, but I knew that the State's evidence was woefully inadequate to prove his guilt beyond a reasonable doubt. Thus, I was actually relieved when the jury returned a verdict of not guilty. The evidence presented was simply not strong enough to justify a conviction. We had not established the defendant's guilt beyond a reasonable doubt —not by a longshot. The system, however, had worked. I did my job. The defense attorney did his. And the jury did theirs.

---

[86] An artist's sketch of the second man led to the arrest of a second suspect, but the charges were later dismissed when the surviving victim was unable to make a positive identification.

[87] Prosecutors don't have the luxury of being agnostic when it comes to the guilt of the accused on trial. The jurors in any given case have every right to expect that the prosecutor trying the case is personally convinced of the defendant's guilt. But see fn. 8.

[88] I had originally announced that the State would seek the death penalty in this case. But the more time I spent analyzing this case – both with respect to the lack of thoroughness of the investigation and the lack of credibility of my witnesses – the more my confidence waned regarding the strength of the case. So, I withdrew my death penalty announcement.

[89] The defense contended that the victim and the deceased had quarreled and that the victim shot his lover in a fit of anger and then wounded himself in a failed attempt to commit suicide.

The William Phelps "$22 Murder" Case[90]

Under Georgia law, the State is not required to prove a murder defendant's motive for killing his victim. The prosecution is only required to prove that a defendant caused the victim's death and, in doing so, had acted with malice aforethought, i.e., with the deliberate intention to kill without justification, excuse, or mitigation.[91] Nonetheless, every prosecutor knows that jurors want to understand the "why" behind a killing. And the "why" is often the most convincing link in establishing the "who." So, most prosecutors will at least attempt to discover what the killer's motive was in order to satisfy the jury's curiosity.

Early one August morning in 1999, a deer hunter stumbled upon the body of a headless man leaning against a tree near a rocky creek bed in a remote wooded area near the border between Newton and Walton Counties.[92] Newton County deputies responded to the scene and summoned a GBI crime scene tech to examine and collect evidence from and around the extensively decomposed body. The deceased man's skull and one arm were located some distance from his body – likely due to "animal activity." The tech noted that the pockets of the man's pants had been "turned out" as if someone had attempted to remove their contents. The collected body parts and clothing were carefully packaged and sent to the GBI Crime Lab where Dr. Mark Koponen performed an autopsy. Dr. Koponen concluded that the cause of death was blunt force trauma and described two distinct blunt

---

[90] Phelps v. State, 278 Ga. 402 (2004).

[91] "Justification" might be self-defense; an "excuse" might be insanity – the inability to distinguish right from wrong; "mitigation" might be a provocation sufficient to reduce the charge to manslaughter.

[92] It was later determined that the victim's body was actually located in Walton County, not Newton County. In order to prove that Walton County was the proper venue for the trial, I was forced to engage the services of a land surveyor!

force injuries to the victim's skull – injuries consistent with the victim having been struck twice in the head with a rock.

The victim was later identified by post-mortem fingerprints as Jeffrey Valdez. This led investigators to question Valdez's acquaintances, including a man named William Phelps and his sister Elizabeth. Elizabeth told police that in July after a night of drinking, Valdez had stayed at her apartment overnight along with her brother William. She further advised that when William woke the next morning, he discovered that $22 was missing from his wallet. William suspected that Valdez had taken his money sometime during the night and told Elizabeth that he intended to confront Valdez as soon as he awakened. But Elizabeth didn't want a fight in her apartment, so she insisted that William confront Valdez about the missing money elsewhere. William agreed.

Elizabeth told investigators that later that day, she, William, and Valdez drove to a hunting preserve near the Phelps' childhood home. She stated that after they had walked approximately a mile down a dirt path, William picked up a rock and struck Valdez repeatedly in the head. She then saw her brother rifle through Valdez's pants pockets looking for his $22, but it wasn't there. She then watched helplessly as Phelps drug Valdez's body deep into the woods and propped him against a tree. Elizabeth believed that Valdez was still alive as she and William walked back to their car. In other words, Valdez was left to die alone in the sweltering summer heat.[93]

Thanks in large part to Elizabeth's testimony against her brother, William Phelps was convicted and sentenced to life imprisonment.

---

[93] On appeal, Phelps didn't dispute Elizabeth's account of the assault but unsuccessfully argued that the State had failed to prove the victim's true cause of death beyond a reasonable doubt.

* * *

The Phelps case illustrates a recurring theme in many criminal prosecutions: Very often, the key witness for the State will be a close relative, friend, or associate of the defendant. In the Phelps case, it was William's sister Elizabeth. I was always somewhat sympathetic to the plight of such witnesses. I had no choice but to subpoena them and force them to testify. But what a horrible dilemma: Testify truthfully and watch your loved one or friend go to prison, or testify falsely, commit perjury, and risk going to prison yourself. Nonetheless, as the early 20th-century legal scholar John Henry Wigmore noted in his treatise on the law of evidence, *Wigmore on Evidence*, "The public is entitled to every man's evidence."[94]

And, as in the Phelps case, every *woman's* evidence as well.

The Jimmy Norton Case[95]

The newspaper headline in the *Rockdale Citizen* read: "I heard my mommy scream."

These chilling words spoken by Melissa Douglas' 4-year-old son would be the centerpiece of one of the most challenging and contentious trials in my career as a prosecutor. Did this poor little boy actually witness his mother's murder? Was she killed by her boyfriend, Jimmy Norton, as contended by the State? Or was she killed by an intruder? A Newton County jury would ultimately answer these questions. But like no other murder case in my almost 14 years as a prosecutor, the

---

[94] See Wigmore, Evidence (3rd) §2192. Prominent exceptions include a defendant's 5th Amendment privilege against being compelled to give testimony against himself and, as discussed in Chapter 6 – Whodunit?, The Randy Peters Case, the spousal testimonial privilege which provides that a person cannot be compelled to testify in a criminal case against his or her spouse.

[95] Norton v. State, 263 Ga. 448 (1993).

outcome of this case would be in doubt right up until the reading of the jury's verdict.

The Norton case got its start in the early 1990s in the small South Georgia town of Vidalia – known as the "Sweet Onion Capital of the World."[96] And I'm sure that the Vidalia Chamber of Commerce was quite pleased with that designation. Unfortunately, Vidalia and the surrounding counties were also known at that time for marijuana smuggling and for the dead bodies that were frequently found dumped in the swamps of South Georgia. So, you might be wondering, what possible connection did the goings-on in Vidalia have to do with my Circuit located 150 miles away in North Georgia? Read on.

Jimmy Norton met and fell head over heels in love with Melissa Douglas,[97] a 19-year-old divorced mother of one, who lived and worked in Vidalia, Georgia. When Jimmy and Melissa began dating, Jimmy was attending Brewton-Parker College in nearby Mount Vernon, Georgia. When not attending to her 4-year-old son, Stephen, Melissa was the bookkeeper for her father's finance company – a business that was quite possibly a front for his illegal drug trafficking operation. Melissa's father, Buddy Williams, you see, happened to be a drug kingpin in the so-called "Dixie Mafia." Dixie Mafia? Yes, you read that correctly. The Dixie Mafia was the Southern version of its better-known Northern relative. It specialized in stolen merchandise, illegal alcohol, and drugs. And like its Northern counterpart, it was not shy about committing extortion, bribery, and murder to attain its goals.

---

[96] According to the 1986 Vidalia Onion Act, no onion grown outside the 20-county area surrounding Vidalia may be called a "Vidalia" onion.

[97] Jimmy's affection for Melissa could more accurately be described as "an obsession." Dozens of apparently unrequited love letters from Jimmy to Melissa were later found and introduced at his trial.

For whatever reason, Melissa's family took an immediate dislike to Jimmy. And their disdain for him only intensified when they learned that Jimmy had been freelancing with the Vidalia Police Department as an undercover drug snitch. Suffice it to say, Jimmy's relationship with the Vidalia P.D. and Buddy's drug trafficking operation posed, well, shall we say, an awkward conflict of interest. So, in an attempt to scare Jimmy off, the family enlisted one of Buddy's associates and one of Mellissa's former boyfriends to rough Jimmy up a bit. And when Jimmy attempted to run away from this beat down, one of the men shot Jimmy in the buttocks. Although Jimmy was not seriously hurt, he was justifiably scared. Ironically, Melissa, who had also grown tired of Jimmy, now felt sorry for him and took him back. The family's plan had, well, backfired.

As it turned out, this shooting incident came at a bad time for the Drug Enforcement Administration (DEA) – not to mention Jimmy's buttocks. At the time, the DEA had just arrested Buddy Williams for drug smuggling and he had agreed to cooperate with the DEA in its undercover investigation of the Dixie Mafia – code-named "Operation Zulu." Okay. I know. At this point, some of you are thinking that I'm making this s--- up. I'm not. I swear that this is a true story. Read on.

Fearing that this dust-up between Jimmy and Buddy's Dixie Mafia associates might interfere with its ongoing investigation, the DEA offered Jimmy and Melissa a few hundred dollars to move away from the Onion Capital and to lie low for a while. Thus, the couple, along with Melissa's son, Stephen, moved 150 miles north to the Fieldcrest Apartments in Newton County. Jimmy would later claim that he and Melissa had been placed in the "Witness Protection Program." This wasn't true. But Jimmy was prone to exaggeration. The truth is: the DEA never considered the couple to be in any serious danger. And apparently, neither did Jimmy nor Melissa, for neither changed their names or otherwise attempted to conceal their identities. Jimmy got a job at a popular restaurant in nearby Conyers. And both continued to visit with their families on a regular basis.

Tragically, however, within a few short months of their relocation to my Circuit, Melissa would be dead.

Not long after their move to Newton County, Melissa's relationship with Jimmy began to falter once again and Melissa began making plans to reunite with her ex-husband, Greg, Stephen's father.[98] One night in February of 1992, while talking with her sister Michelle on the phone in the master bedroom, Melissa made a fatal mistake: She told Michelle about her plans to leave Jimmy. Unbeknownst to Melissa, Jimmy was listening to this conversation on the extension phone in the living room.[99] Jimmy was incensed. He was not about to let Melissa dump him for her ex-husband – not after all her family had put him through.

When Melissa hung up the phone and emerged from the master bedroom, Jimmy immediately confronted her about her no-longer-secret plans to leave him and a loud argument ensued. When Melissa attempted to seek refuge in the bedroom, Jimmy grabbed a kitchen knife from a butcher block in the kitchen and pursued her. His intentions were clear: If he couldn't have Melissa, no one else would. When Jimmy caught up to Melissa, he shoved her onto the bed and proceeded to stab her repeatedly in the chest. The rapidity of Jimmy's furious knife attack cast blood spatter all over the walls and ceiling of the master bedroom.

---

[98] Greg Douglas would later testify at Norton's trial that he and Melissa had discussed plans to reunite the week prior to her murder.

[99] Prior to the cell phone era, most residences had a "land line" telephone with multiple extension phones that shared the same incoming and outgoing calls.

Stephen, who had already been put to bed, was awakened by Jimmy and Melissa's loud argument. He crawled out of his bed, opened his bedroom door, and stood at the door of his mommy's bedroom. It was there that he probably witnessed his mother being stabbed to death. At some point during the attack, Jimmy caught a glimpse of Stephen and angrily told Stephen to "go to bed!" Jimmy then proceeded to finish what he had started. He stood over Melissa's lifeless body and pulled the knife blade across her neck several times – nearly decapitating her. But before leaving the bedroom, he stopped to drape the bedspread over Melissa's ashen face.

So, just how brutal was this knife attack? According to the autopsy report, one of the knife wounds to Melissa's chest was a deep, twisting stab to her heart which was alone sufficient to cause her death. If ending Melissa's life was Jimmy's objective, a single stab was all that was necessary to kill her. But Jimmy didn't just stab Melissa once, he stabbed her over 15 times! Only the cuts to her neck occurred postmortem. No, Jimmy wanted to do more than just kill Melissa, he wanted to vent his anger and rage.

Now what? Jimmy had just sadistically butchered the woman he claimed to love, and he had done so in his own apartment. The crime scene was a bloody mess. There was no way that he could clean the bedroom and conceal Melissa's death. He needed a plan. And he needed one quick. So, shortly before midnight, he quietly slipped out of the apartment with the murder weapon[100] and his bloody clothes[101]

---

[100] Norton actually took and disposed of the entire butcher block knife set. Had he only discarded the one, bloody knife from the butcher block set, it would have been obvious to police that the crime had been committed with a "weapon of opportunity" – likely by someone living in the apartment. Which, of course, was exactly what had happened!

[101] Several witnesses said that Jimmy had been wearing a distinctive maroon-colored work shirt earlier that evening – a shirt that has never been found.

and proceeded to drive to Conyers, Georgia, to dispose of these items and to set up his alibi. And in so doing, he left Stephen home alone in the same apartment with his mother's bloody corpse.

Arriving in Conyers just after midnight, Jimmy met first with his ex-girlfriend Janell in a supermarket parking lot. He told Janell that he and Melissa had argued that night and that he no longer wanted to be with her – that he wanted to rekindle his relationship with her. Then, Jimmy drove to his parents' house. There, Jimmy spoke with one of his brothers who was leaning out of a bedroom window on the second floor. But then, Jimmy made a crucial mistake – the kind of mistake that criminals often make when attempting to fabricate the "perfect alibi." He stopped at a Chevron Station on the way back to his apartment, pumped $3.00 worth of gasoline, and insisted that the convenience store clerk give him a time-stamped receipt – proof that he was in Conyers at the time of the murder – or so he would later claim.

Upon returning to the apartment at around 1:28 a.m., Jimmy attempted to fake a forcible entry through the back door of his apartment,[102] dialed 911, and "frantically" reported that his apartment had been broken into. When the police arrived, Jimmy was sitting in the breakfast room adjacent to the alleged point of entry. He timidly pointed the officers in the direction of the master bedroom. There, the officers discovered Melissa's body covered in blood and nearly decapitated. It was a shocking and unnerving sight – even for experienced police officers. The officers were relieved, however, when they found Stephen unharmed and sound asleep in the adjacent bedroom.

---

[102] According to legendary GBI crime scene analyst Sam House, the physical evidence suggested that the back door had been "pulled in," not kicked in. There were no visible shoe prints, dents, or toolmarks on the exterior of the back door. And the only fingerprints found on the inside doorknob and door jamb were Jimmy's.

After absorbing the initial shock of what they had seen, the officers returned to the rear of the apartment and asked Jimmy if he could explain what had happened. Jimmy, as he had no doubt rehearsed over and over in his head, opened his wallet and showed them the time-stamped gasoline receipt "proving" that he was in Conyers at the time of the "break-in." To say the least, the officers were skeptical. Who gets and keeps a receipt for $3 worth of gasoline? When the sun rose the next morning, little Stephen was in the temporary custody of the Department of Family & Children Services, and as for Jimmy, he was charged with Melissa's murder and in the custody of the police.

Not long after Jimmy's arrest, police investigators got what they thought was a major break in the case. Jimmy's friend and co-worker Jessie Burnette came forward to tell police that he had actually witnessed the murder! He claimed that he had been staying at Jimmy and Melissa's apartment the previous weekend and had returned that night to retrieve a pair of blue jeans that he had inadvertently left behind. At Jimmy's preliminary hearing, Burnette testified as follows:

Jimmy had told him that he suspected that Melissa and Greg were plotting something behind his back and that he would rather see Melissa dead than see her go back with Greg. When he returned to the apartment on the night of the murder, he saw Jimmy follow Melissa into the master bedroom. He then heard Jimmy and Melissa arguing loudly before hearing Melissa emit a "low squealing noise." Thinking that Melissa might be in trouble, he entered the bedroom only to witness Jimmy standing over Melissa and stabbing her repeatedly in the chest with a large knife. He claimed that he tried to stop Jimmy, but that Jimmy fought him off and glared at him with a "devil-like expression" on his face. He claimed that he quickly left the apartment with the intention of calling the police, but didn't because he was afraid of what Jimmy might do to *him* if he did.

Okay, now we had an eyewitness. Or did we? Before the trial, Burnette recanted his statement and said that he had made the whole story up! He claimed that he had succumbed to police pressure to provide damning evidence against Jimmy and simply exercised his very active imagination. So, I was faced with two possibilities: Burnette had either lied (under oath) at the preliminary hearing or he was lying now.[103] To this day, I'm not sure which is true. Because of Burnette's recantation, however, I decided that I could not call him as a witness at Jimmy's trial. In fact, it would have been unethical for me to have done so since I could not discount the strong possibility that Burnette would commit perjury (again).[104] So, when I rested the State's case without having called Burnette as a witness, the newspaper reporters were dumbfounded. How could I fail to call the only "eyewitness" to the crime! Of course, they didn't know about Burnette's recantation and I couldn't tell them about it until the trial was over.

As I mentioned previously, this was a highly contentious case. Now for the contentious part. Jimmy, unlike most of my murder suspects, grew up in a solid, middle-class family. His father was a respected insurance agent in nearby Conyers who had powerful friends including the Sheriff of Rockdale County, Guy Norman. The Norton family was not about to stand idly by and watch one of their own go down without a fight. Thus, before all was said and done, Mr. Norton and his family would attempt to vilify every person associated with the criminal justice system in Newton County.

Now, understandably, Jimmy's father did not want to accept the possibility that his son, Jimmy, might have done the horrendous thing

---

[103] There was actually a third possibility: Burnette could have been the killer. But I didn't think this was likely given that he had no motive to kill Melissa.

[104] Following the trial, I indicted Burnette for felony perjury. He later pled guilty and was sentenced to 6 months in a Diversion Center.

that he was being accused of. So, like any loving parent, he attempted to provide the best legal defense that he could for his son. For starters, he hired a psychologist to testify at Jimmy's bond hearing. And, not surprisingly, his well-paid expert testified that Jimmy posed no significant flight risk or harm to the public if released on bond. I countered this testimony with a State psychologist who, in addition to interviewing Jimmy, also examined items seized from Jimmy's apartment including a shelf full of satanic figurines and a stack of Jimmy's Grim Reaper drawings. Yep. That's what I said – the Grim Reaper, the personification of death. Passing fancy? Nope. Jimmy also had tattoos of the Grim Reaper on his upper arms and back! (Again, I'm not making this stuff up. I still have the photos.) The State's psychologist thus concluded that Jimmy was *not* a good bond risk. Judge Ott agreed and denied bond. As a result, Jimmy would remain in jail until his trial.

And that's when the Norton family declared war. The Nortons soon launched a publicity campaign the likes of which I had never seen before – or since. Jimmy held press conferences at the jail to profess his innocence. And Jimmy's father, who accused Judge Ott and me of attempting to "railroad" Jimmy, began holding daily sandwich-board protests on the Courthouse steps. The Norton family even sponsored a freaking "Jimmy Norton Freedom Fund Benefit" that included a dinner[105] and a golf tournament to raise money for Jimmy's defense!

The Norton family's attacks on Judge Ott, the Covington P.D., and me were relentless. And Jimmy was all in. For example, whenever Jimmy was brought to court for pretrial motion hearings, he would carry a spiral notebook with the words "F--- Cook, F---Capt. Turner," etc. written in bold letters on the front. And Jimmy would make sure that I saw this notebook when he was brought in and out

---

[105] Complete with door prizes including the Grand Prize of a full-length mink coat valued at $6500.

of the courtroom. Moreover, the jail intercepted several letters between Jimmy and his brothers that contained not-so-veiled threats directed at me and Captain Turner.[106]

You might be wondering at this point: Where was the "challenge" that I spoke of previously. Jealous boyfriend kills girlfriend, right? Well, Jimmy's guilt wasn't as clear-cut as it first appeared. Soon after his arrest, Jimmy began floating a seemingly preposterous theory that Melissa's murder was a "drug retaliation hit." Poppycock, we thought, until we learned that Melissa's father, Buddy Williams, had been arrested and charged in Operation Zulu and had agreed to testify against his Dixie Mafia co-conspirators.[107] Was it possible that someone in the Dixie Mafia carried out a "hit" on Melissa to send a message to Buddy to keep his mouth shut?

To find out, lead investigator Captain Almond Turner and I drove to Brunswick to interview Buddy Williams at a federal holding facility. Williams told us that no one had threatened him or his family – including Melissa, and that no one had contacted him to claim responsibility for Melissa's murder. He was firmly convinced that Jimmy was the killer. But would a jury be so sure? Captain Turner and I were worried. Jimmy was a handsome young man from a middle-class family. He was represented by a very good, well-liked local attorney.[108] There was a very real possibility that Jimmy might be able to convince a

---

[106] The Norton brothers were later visited by law enforcement agents from the NCIS, the GBI, and the local police. I was told that the older brother was taken off a Navy vessel in the Mediterranean, read the riot act, and sternly warned to knock it off. Similar warnings were given to Norton's younger brother. By that time, however, I had already purchased my first firearm, a S&W .38, and carried it for several years thereafter.

[107] Williams had been arrested in possession of large quantities of cocaine and marijuana.

[108] Jimmy's attorney was Samuel D. "Sammy" Ozburn. Ozburn was a successful and respected solo practitioner with strong ties to the community. In a close case, the jury could easily have been swayed by Ozburn's reputation alone.

jury that reasonable doubt existed as to his guilt. We needed more. We needed something to convince a jury that Jimmy's "hit" theory didn't hold water. And fortunately, we found it.

When Captain Turner alerted me to the growing use of criminal profilers in whodunit cases, we decided to drive to Savannah to attend a lecture by FBI profiler Gregg McCrary.[109] After serving in various investigative capacities throughout the United States, Agent McCrary had joined the FBI profiler unit at Quantico, Virginia. At this specialized unit, Agent McCrary analyzed crimes and crime scenes and constructed behavioral profiles of unknown offenders. He was also one of the contributing authors of the FBI's *Crime Classification Manual*.[110]

After Agent McCrary's lecture, Capt. Turner and I met with him, and he graciously agreed to review our case file and provide his expert opinion. Our question to him was simple: Was it possible that Melissa's murder was a "drug retaliation hit?" Several weeks later, Agent McCrary rendered his expert opinion: Based upon solid statistical data compiled in the *Crime Classification Manual* and his own personal experience investigating homicides, Agent McCrary concluded that Melissa's murder was consistent with a "domestic rage homicide," *not* a professional hit.

Agent McCrary explained that hitmen don't use weapons of opportunity – like kitchen knives; they use small caliber pistols. And they don't engage in "overkill" – like 15 stab wounds; they direct one

---

[109] The drive home from Savannah on I-16 proved memorable. Capt. Turner was driving 90 mph in a Ford Crown Victoria with a "police package," i.e., it had a souped-up engine. From a distance, I caught a faint glimpse of a buzzard feasting on roadkill. But in a matter of seconds, car and carrion attempted to occupy the same molecular space. The buzzard would have had a better chance of survival against a Randy Johnson fastball. See https://www.youtube.com/watch?v=qwpRHrAh3pk

[110] Agent McCrary is also the author of a fascinating book on serial killers titled *The Unknown Darkness, Profiling the Predators Among Us*. I highly recommend it.

or two well-placed shots to the victim's head. By comparison, Agent McCrary pointed out, domestic rage homicides frequently involve *both* weapons of opportunity and overkill. Moreover, Agent McCrary also noted the prevalence of "undoing" in domestic rage homicides – where the perpetrator attempts to distance himself from what he has done. In our case, the "undoing" was Jimmy's draping of the bedspread over Melissa's face after the attack. A hitman would not have shown such remorse, regret, or revulsion at what he had done.

After receiving Agent McCrary's report, I called and asked him if he would be willing to provide his expert testimony at Jimmy's trial. He agreed – at *no* cost to us. Having secured Agent McCrary's commitment to testify, I felt confident that we would be able to convince a jury to reject Jimmy's Dixie Mafia hitman theory. But reasonable doubt is a high bar, and I knew that we might need more to convince the jury that it was in fact Jimmy who had wielded the knife. I concluded that the centerpiece – the lynchpin if you will – to winning this case was likely going to be the videotape of the interview of 4-year-old Stephen Douglas made on the day after the murder. His words and actions in this video were chilling – and accusatory. At one point during his videotaped interview, he made a stabbing motion with his hand while saying, "Jimmy hurt my momma, Jimmy hurt my momma."

I simply had to find a way to show Stephen's videotaped interview to the jury. The problem was that under the rules of evidence, Stephen's videotaped interview was inadmissible hearsay. Moreover, even if I could have cited an exception to the hearsay rule, the Sixth Amendment's Confrontation Clause would still have barred the admission of the videotape unless I first provided the defense with an opportunity to cross-examine Stephen. So, I had no choice – I had to call Stephen as a witness at Norton's trial.

My challenge was to call Stephen as a witness in the least trau-
matic way possible. Toward that end, I reached an agreement with
Norton's attorney to permit Stephen to testify via closed-circuit TV
from a room adjacent to the courtroom.[111] But as if to add one last rung
to an already tall ladder, circumstances forced me to call Stephen after
lunch when he was visibly drowsy and in need of a nap. As a result, my
initial attempts to question him on direct examination failed miserably.
Fortunately, on re-direct, as if he had been given a shot of adrenaline,
Stephen suddenly came to life and testified to his vivid memories of
that night. Among other things, he described hearing his mommy and
Jimmy "hollering real loud" and hearing "his mommy scream." And
critically, because I had made Stephen available for cross-examination,
I was then able to play Stephen's original videotaped interview to a rapt
audience in the jury box – and with devastating effect.[112]

After seven days of trial, the jury returned a verdict of guilty.

* * *

I had always instructed my ADAs to calmly and professionally read the
jury's verdict without showing any emotion regardless of the verdict –
guilty or not guilty. And I did so in this case. But as soon as the jury
was released, I, Capt. Turner and the other Covington P.D. officers
who had worked on this case so tirelessly and who had been, like Capt.
Turner and me, so maligned by the Norton family, made our way to

---

[111] I suspect that Jimmy agreed to waive his right to a face-to-face courtroom confrontation
because he feared that the jury's ability to see Stephen's live, in-court testimony might be even
more damaging.

[112] Stephen's videotaped statement became admissible, in part, because Jimmy's attorney had
accused Stephen's father, Greg, on cross-examination of poisoning Stephen's mind against Jimmy
in the months leading up to the trial. But because Stephen's videotaped statement was given *on
the day after the murder*, it became admissible as a so-called "prior consistent statement" to rebut
Jimmy's claim of *recent* influence.

the basement of the Courthouse where the District Attorney's Office was located. But I must admit, the celebration started well before we made it to the bottom of the steps. I had never before or since experienced such revelry of man hugs, high-fives, and congratulatory whooping and hollering. It was probably the most exhilarating experience in my 35 years of practicing law.

* * *

And, oh, by the way, following Jimmy's failed appeal, he finally confessed to his father that he had in fact killed Melissa.

CHAPTER 4

Hiring a Hitman

If you are like me, you probably watch a lot of real-life crime shows like NBC'S *Dateline* or ABC's *20/20*. These shows have featured many episodes in which a spouse (or significant other) has attempted to hire a hitman to dispose of their partner. More often than not, however, they end up negotiating the "hit" with an undercover police officer. And almost invariably, they are caught on videotape discussing the plot and, not infrequently, handing over the down-payment! In such scenarios, all a prosecutor needs to do in order to prove "criminal attempt to commit murder" is show that the defendant took a "substantial step" toward the commission of the crime, e.g., making the aforementioned down-payment.

In the preceding chapter, you read about the Jimmy Norton case in which the defendant denied murdering his girlfriend and claimed instead that she had been killed by a hitman hired by the Dixie Mafia. In that case, the jury rejected Norton's claim and concluded that there was no hitman and that Norton had committed the murder himself. In this chapter, however, I'll describe two cases in which there really was a hitman.

In a true hitman case when the "hit" is actually carried out, a prosecutor will usually have little difficulty in assessing the relative culpability of the two main actors: the person who hired the hitman and the person who carried out the "hit." This is because *both* individuals are legally responsible for the victim's death – the latter being the "principle" and the former being a "party to the crime." Consequently, both individuals are subject to the same penalty: death or life imprisonment. A different assessment might take place, however, if the alleged hitman backs out and refuses to carry out the "hit." This is especially true if the hitman alerts authorities to the existence of the plot and agrees to cooperate with them. And that is what happened in the two cases described below.

The Wayne Parham Case[113]

Did you ever wonder why the husband (or ex-husband) immediately becomes the prime suspect when a wife (or ex-wife) goes missing or turns up dead? Well, there's a good reason. Experience tells us that most women who are killed as a result of foul play not only know their attacker – they were probably married to him![114] And if the husband (or ex-husband) is reluctant to do the dirty deed himself, he often attempts to hire a hitman.

Wayne Parham hated his ex-wife – and the feeling was mutual. Parham, who had remarried, was involved in a bitter custody fight with his ex-wife. While in the throes of this legal battle, he began dropping not-so-subtle hints to a friend that he wanted his ex-wife "done away with completely." Before long, he told this friend point-blank that he was willing to pay money to have his ex-wife killed and asked the friend to find someone to do the job. Parham was aware of the fact that his friend "knew people" in Walton County – the kind of people who killed

---

[113] Parham v. State, A97A2117, September 25, 1997 (not officially reported).

[114] For a twist on this theme, see Chapter 6 – Whodunit Cases, The Randy Peters Case, where the wife was the one accused of having her husband killed.

people for money.[115] Soon thereafter, the friend made contact with an honest-to-God hitman and negotiated a "contract" on Parham's behalf. The hitman was later provided with a down payment, a shotgun, a photograph of the ex-wife, and directions to the ex-wife's home.

Before the hitman could perform his end of the bargain, however, he was arrested on unrelated charges. Perhaps looking for a deal, he spilled his guts to police about this murder-for-hire plot. He claimed, of course, that he never intended to actually kill anyone – he was just going to take the money and run. So, he was quite willing to name the other parties to the contract: Parham and his friend. And when investigators questioned Parham's friend, surprisingly, he told them the entire sordid story. The investigators were, quite frankly, taken aback by his candor. Apparently, Parham's friend was unaware that the middleman in a murder-for-hire plot could be charged as a "party to the crime" – even if the intended killing never took place. Amazingly, other Parham family and friends also gave statements to police admitting that they had overheard Parham talking about "offing" his ex-wife. As a result, both Parham and his friend were charged with criminal attempt to solicit murder.

When this case came to trial in early 1996, everyone except the putative hitman changed their stories. They claimed that the whole thing was just a big joke – that no one had actually been serious about killing anyone. Extracting the truth from these witnesses was, well, like pulling teeth. (My wife, a former dentist, swears that pulling teeth isn't really all that difficult – apparently, it's all in the wrists.) As a consequence, I was forced to impeach almost every one of these witnesses by confronting them with their original inculpatory statements to police.

---

[115] The "people" Parham's friend knew were (and remain) suspects in The Randy Peters Case. See Chapter 6.

But the real key to proving my case rested upon the much-anticipated testimony of the alleged hitman. And, boy, did he deliver. Tattooed up one side and down the other, he definitely looked the part. (As they say in Hollywood, he looked like he had been hired right out of Central Casting.) To drive home the point, I made no attempt to hide the fact that the alleged hitman was presently incarcerated. In fact, I insisted that he testify in his State Prison uniform. The jury sat mesmerized as they listening to the putative hitman's sterile, business-like description of "the arrangement." And yet, the jury was also visibly uncomfortable being seated so closely to him. Ironically, it was the hitman who the jury found most credible as they voted to convict.

* * *

We had an unusually large audience for the Parham trial. The ex-wife and her divorce lawyer, both of whom had more than a casual interest in the outcome, attended daily. And the defendant's family and friends were also well-represented. This made for quite the spectacle when the guilty verdict was read. Parham's new wife went berserk and had to be carried out of the courtroom by deputies. Ordinarily, her conduct would have resulted in contempt of court charges, but the trial judge let it slide. Her husband, on the other hand, was sentenced to prison.

* * *

Ironically, this wasn't the last time that I would see Parham's wife. Later that year, when I was running for re-election, I noticed that she was seated on the front row at a political forum. She was there to support my opponent in the 1996 district attorney race – her husband's defense attorney, Stan Cox! If dirty looks could kill, I would have been out of the race and Mr. Cox would have won in a cakewalk. But they can't and he didn't.

The Clyde Putnam Case

Not long after trying the Parham case, I prosecuted yet another hitman case. Change the names and move the venue to Newton County and you have the Clyde Putnam case. Putnam was a divorced optician who, like Parham, wanted his ex-wife dead. And like the Parham case, his hitman of choice also backed out and ratted him out to police.

Unlike the Parham case, however, this case would ultimately be resolved with a guilty plea. But like the Parham case, Putnam's new wife would play a key role in the drama surrounding the prosecution. In a most unusual move, I agreed to permit the new Mrs. Putnam, Priscilla (not her real name), to testify before the grand jury. She swore to me that she had highly relevant information to share with the grand jury that would prove her husband's innocence. So, I reluctantly agreed. (And, frankly, I wanted to know what she had to say so I wouldn't get blindsided by her testimony if the case went to trial.)

When it was Priscilla's turn to testify, she entered the grand jury room clutching something tightly to her chest. After placing her under oath, I asked her what she wanted to tell the grand jury. And that's when she revealed the object that she had been holding: It was a framed, glossy, 8x10 color photograph of the happy couple and their two young children. Can you say, "sympathy play?" I had been had. She had played me like a violin. So, mustering up the last morsel of my dignity, I calmly walked to the door, asked the grand jury bailiff to step inside, and instructed him to, "Get her out of here!" I won't say that she had to be dragged out, but she didn't exactly go quietly either. True to form, however, that would not be the last time that we would hear from Priscilla.

Putnam eventually pled guilty to conspiracy to commit murder and received a 5-year prison sentence.[116] The judge, however, permitted Putnam to get his affairs in order before he was required to report to jail to begin serving his sentence. On the appointed day, Priscilla dutifully drove her husband to the Newton County jail. Upon their arrival, however, they were unexpectantly greeted by a photographer from the *Covington News* who was there to capture the moment on film - what we used to call before digital photography, a *Kodak* moment. This apparently infuriated Priscilla, and she proceeded to grab the photographer's camera, retreat to her car, and lock herself inside. Responding deputies later persuaded Priscilla to relinquish the camera, but its roll of film had "mysteriously" disappeared.

The Randy Peters Case

See CHAPTER 6 – Whodunit Cases, The Randy Peters Case.

---

[116] The alleged hitman also pled guilty and received a 2-year prison sentence.

CHAPTER 5

Prosecutorial Discretion

Prosecutors stand in a unique position in the American criminal justice system. Prosecutors are responsible for ensuring that innocents are protected – an obligation that includes wrongfully accused persons as well as crime victims. In carrying out this responsibility, prosecutors have the power and the duty in the exercise of their sound "prosecutorial discretion" to carefully screen out weak or inconsequential cases.[117] And in the exercise of this discretion, prosecutors are not beholden to police, politicians, judges, or even crime victims; their only allegiance is to the law, truth, common sense, and public safety.

I would often tell my law students, "In my *heart*, I never prosecuted an innocent person, but in my *head*, I know that I probably did." What I was trying to convey to them was that although I endeavored to use my best professional judgment in every case to avoid prosecuting an innocent person, I – like all human beings – was capable of making mistakes.[118] This is part of the reason why during my years as a prose-

---

[117] It has been said that there are so many criminal laws on the books that if a prosecutor had enough time and resources, he or she could prosecute nearly everyone for something. Fortunately, in our system, a prosecutor may decline to prosecute a case – despite being legally entitled to do so – when neither public policy nor community safety warrants such a prosecution.

[118] I have absolutely no reason to believe, however, that any of the defendants that I tried and who were convicted by a jury were factually innocent, and no appellate court - state or federal – has

cutor, I truly appreciated the role played by competent, ethical defense attorneys. These attorneys would occasionally come to me and point out inconsistencies in my evidence and other weaknesses in my cases that I hadn't noticed. This enabled me to exercise my prosecutorial discretion more judiciously.

Thus, the true beauty of the American criminal justice system is that it doesn't depend upon the judgment of any single individual. Multiple and often redundant safeguards exist to reduce the possibility that an innocent person will suffer a wrongful conviction. Consider this:

> A police officer must have probable cause to make a warrantless arrest. That police officer must then convince a judicial officer that there was, in fact, sufficient probable cause to justify the warrantless arrest. If the arrestee isn't granted bail or cannot make bond, he is entitled to a preliminary hearing at which he may contest these previous probable cause determinations before yet another judicial officer. If the charge is a felony, the arrestee may not be prosecuted unless indicted by a grand jury – yet another probable cause finding, this time made by 23 citizens selected randomly from the community. Then, if the accused demands a jury trial, a six or twelve-person jury must find him guilty beyond a reasonable doubt. And if he is convicted, he may pursue multiple levels of appeals in both the state and federal appellate courts.[119]

---

ever concluded otherwise.

[119] The number of decision-makers involved in this process is mindboggling. By my count, if a convicted defendant's case were to be appealed through both the state and federal systems, well over 70 individuals – including police officers and prosecutors, magistrate judges and trial judges, grand jurors and trial jurors, and appellate judges and justices – would play a role in assessing the defendant's legal rights and factual guilt.

All of these safeguards exist *in addition to* a prosecutor's wise use of his or her prosecutorial discretion.

Do wrongful convictions occur? Yes. But the news media and Hollywood exaggerate the extent to which this occurs. This is particularly true with respect to death penalty cases. If you watch shows like CNN'S *Death Penalty Stories*, you'd think that every death row inmate was framed, entrapped, railroaded, bamboozled, steamrolled, hoodwinked, or worse. What these critics of the system won't tell you is that even when a conviction is reversed on appeal, it doesn't necessarily mean that the defendant was innocent of the crime charged.[120] Most reversals are predicated, not on proof that the defendant was wrongfully accused, but on legal errors that rendered his trial unfair. In such cases, due process and fundamental fairness demand that the defendant gets a new trial – a second bite at the apple. But more often than not, the defendant in such cases either pleads guilty to a lesser offense and/or receives a lesser sentence, or is convicted again upon retrial.

Thus, the problem with most wrongful conviction claims is that they disingenuously equate a reversal due to legal errors with factual innocence. The two are far from the same. A factually guilty drug trafficker, for example, will be freed from prison if an appellate court determines that his illicit drugs were illegally seized and improperly admitted into evidence at his trial. In that scenario, the drug trafficker will go free, but he was not wrongfully accused, and he was assuredly not "innocent."

Another fundamental misconception is that our criminal justice system can "exonerate" a wrongfully accused person. It can convict the guilty. And it can acquit those found not guilty. But it cannot proclaim

---

[120] Justice Thomas dissects these misleading claims in Kansas v. Marsh, 548 U.S. 163, 180, and n. 7 (2006).

a person's innocence.[121] Of course, this is truly unfortunate in a case in which an accused was, in fact, innocent of the charges against him. As former Reagan Administration Labor Secretary Raymond Donovan once famously said after his acquittal on corruption charges, "To which office do I go to get my reputation back?"

This inability of the system to exonerate the wrongfully accused highlights the importance of prosecutors exercising extreme care in making their prosecutorial decisions. As I told my ADAs and students on many occasions, a prosecutor cannot be "agnostic" when it comes to his or her assessment of an accused's guilt. If a prosecutor isn't firmly convinced of an accused's guilt, he or she cannot ethically ask a jury to convict. He or she must decline to prosecute the case.

The following case is a good example of why the criminal justice system typically cannot exonerate those who claim to have been wrongfully accused.

The Willie Frank Williams Case

A 62-year-old woman in Loganville, Georgia, had been raped in her home. Police developed a suspect named Willie Frank Williams who, after a lengthy interrogation, confessed to the crime. Williams told his court-appointed attorney, Marvin Sorrells, however, that his confession had been coerced. Nonetheless, this claim was rejected by the trial judge and Williams' confession was ruled admissible. Sorrells thus pleaded with Williams to take the stand at his trial to explain to the jury why

---

[121] To illustrate this point, one need look no further than the infamous O. J. Simpson cases. A criminal jury acquitted Simpson of murdering his ex-wife Nicole Brown Simpson and her male friend Ron Goldman. In that case, as with all acquittals in criminal cases, the jury found that the prosecution had failed to prove its case beyond a reasonable doubt. A civil jury in a subsequent wrongful death lawsuit filed by Goldman's family, however, found by a preponderance of the evidence that Simpson had in fact killed Goldman and assaulted Nicole. Moreover, the vast majority of Americans still believe that Simpson committed both of these heinous murders.

he had given a false confession. But, according to Sorrells, Williams refused to testify because he was deathly afraid of being cross-examined by District Attorney John Ott.

Aside from his confession, the evidence against Williams was almost entirely circumstantial.[122] The victim had blacked out during the attack and could not describe her attacker. And while Williams' fingerprints were not found anywhere in the victim's home, there was an unidentified latent fingerprint on the inside of the victim's back door. Williams' conviction, therefore, was based largely on his detailed confession to the crime.[123] Jurors would later say that Williams' decision not to take the stand and refute his confession led to their decision to convict.[124]

Fast-forward four years later. Loganville Police Chief Eddie Sharpe, who was never convinced that Williams committed this crime, had periodically run the unidentified print in this case against the AFIS[125] database. One day, he got a hit. The unidentified fingerprint belonged to a man named Echols whose fingerprints had been recently entered into AFIS in an unrelated case. And when questioned about the old rape case, Echols (also) confessed to the crime!

---

[122] Defense attorneys love to deride circumstantial evidence. But cases built on circumstantial evidence can be extremely strong. Example: A burglary suspect is arrested within minutes after the burglary just two blocks from the victim's home in possession of burglar tools and the home-owner's unique diamond necklace. Defense attorney: "But no one actually saw him commit the burglary – the evidence is purely circumstantial!" Would you vote to convict on this "purely circumstantial" evidence? I would.

[123] False confessions are rare, but they are well-documented. For this reason, Georgia law requires that a suspect's confession must be corroborated. See O.C.G.A. §24-8-823.

[124] Although jurors are instructed not to penalize a defendant for exercising his 5th Amendment privilege against self-incrimination, as a practical matter, many jurors simply can't ignore it when a defendant refuses to take the stand to defend himself.

[125] AFIS stands for "Automated Fingerprint Identification System."

By the time this new evidence surfaced, however, Ott was no longer the District Attorney and Sorrells was no longer an attorney in private practice – both were by that time Superior Court judges. I was the District Attorney by then and it would be my job to sort this mess out. Clearly, something was amiss. So, when Loganville mayor and attorney Mike Jones filed an Extraordinary Motion for New Trial on Williams' behalf, not only did I not contest his motion, I joined Jones in securing Williams' release from prison on a consent bond pending further investigation.

But what I learned next gave me pause. It turned out that Williams and Echols had been "running buddies" at the time of the rape. Was it possible that both Echols *and* Williams had taken part in this rape?[126] After all, the victim had blacked out during the crime and might not have been aware that a second man was also present in her home. To find out, I asked the GBI Crime Lab to compare Williams' DNA to the sample collected in the victim's rape kit.[127] Unfortunately, the Crime Lab's DNA analyst informed me that the sample from the rape kit was too degraded to enable the Crime Lab to reach a definitive conclusion.[128]

After a thorough examination of the available evidence, I concluded that it was still possible that Williams had been a party to this crime. Thus, despite requests by Williams' attorney and Chief Sharpe

---

[126] Echols maintained that he acted alone. But could he have been covering for Williams, his "running buddy," who could have ratted him out 4 years earlier, but didn't?

[127] At the time of the original trial, DNA technology had not been readily available or capable of making a definitive comparison of known and unknown samples.

[128] Moreover, even if Williams' DNA hadn't matched the rape kit sample, there were numerous possible explanations for this other than his factual innocence, e.g., he might not have ejaculated, he might have worn a condom, or Echols might have committed the rape while Williams acted as a lookout – thus, still a party to the crime. But see fn. 8.

– and the Atlanta news media[129] eager to expose a "wrongful" conviction, I could not officially exonerate Williams. On the other hand, Echol's confession clearly created reasonable doubts about Williams' guilt. Thus, I elected to dismiss the charges against Williams rather than retry him. He was a free man once more. But innocent? Only he knows.

---

[129] I gave TV interviews to Channels 2 and 5 during this controversy - in the midst of my first campaign for office.

CHAPTER 6

Whodunit Cases

In the board game *Clue*, players gather clues regarding the murder of one of the game's colorful characters, including Miss Scarlet, Mr. Green, Colonel Mustard, and Professor Plum. The object of the game is to identify the killer, the murder weapon, and the location where the murder took place, e.g., Mrs. Peacock, with the Lead Pipe, in the Dining Room. This task is accomplished by a process of elimination because in the game, unlike real life, there are a finite number of possible suspects, weapons, and crime scenes to choose from, i.e., a limited number of permutations.

In real life, however, such "whodunits"[130] are considerably more difficult to solve. In fact, whodunits are among the most challenging cases that law enforcement officers and prosecutors must contend with. You have a crime. You have a victim. And maybe you have a suspect or two – or maybe you don't. The victim's family expects the police to make a quick arrest. But police can't just arrest anyone. And

---

[130] The term "whodunit" was coined in 1930 by a book reviewer named Donald Gordon to distinguish mystery novels from other genres.

prosecutors can't just prosecute anyone. They have to arrest and prosecute the *right* one.[131]

The percentage of unsolved homicides in this country is on the rise. Why? Expert criminalists blame this trend on the growing number of so-called "stranger-on-stranger" crimes – homicides in which the perpetrator targets a person that he doesn't know. This lack of connection between the victim and the perpetrator makes it extremely difficult for law enforcement to narrow the pool of potential suspects.[132] And that poses an often impossible task for already overworked investigators. In recent years, however, with the advent of more sophisticated forensic tools like mitochondrial DNA and genetic genealogy,[133] unsolved cases have increasingly become the focus of so-called "cold case" investigations. And some of these cold cases have been successfully prosecuted decades after the crime was committed.

I dealt with many whodunits in my prosecution career, but none more controversial – and frustrating – than the two cases described below.

The Moore's Ford "Mass Lynching" Case

One day in the mid-1990s, an FBI agent dropped by my Walton County office unexpectedly. He asked me if I would be interested in prosecuting a 50-year-old "cold case" involving the lynching of four Black citizens in 1946. As I would soon learn, the shotgun slaying of these four Black citizens is believed to be the last mass lynching in the

---

[131] Police may not lawfully arrest a person unless they have probable cause to believe that such person has committed a crime. And although prosecutors may ethically prosecute a defendant on bare probable cause, most will not try a defendant unless they are firmly convinced of the defendant's guilt and believe that there is a "substantial likelihood of conviction."

[132] See https://www.ncjrs.gov/pdffiles1/jr000243b.pdf

[133] See https://www.nytimes.com/2020/06/29/us/golden-state-killer-joseph-deangelo.html

Old South. The crime was carried out by a mob of White citizens and occurred near the Moore's Ford Bridge on the border between Walton and Oconee Counties. One of the four victims, Roger Malcom, had just bonded out of jail for allegedly stabbing a white man with a knife. Someone apparently tipped off the mob to Malcom's impending release, and Malcom and the others were stopped by the mob just before they reached the Moore's Ford bridge. The mob ordered them out of the car, tied them to an oak tree, and shot them over 60 times at point-blank range.

News of these killings drew national attention, and the resulting outrage led President Truman to create the first President's Committee on Civil Rights. Although these killings did not violate any existing federal criminal statute, President Truman nonetheless ordered the FBI to investigate. The Walton County community, however, was reportedly very tight-lipped and hesitant to cooperate with federal authorities – either because they wanted to protect the wrongdoers or because they feared for their own safety. Unfortunately, after a four-month-long investigation, the FBI was unable to gather sufficient evidence to charge anyone with these horrific crimes. And a subsequent federal grand jury investigation also failed to pull together sufficient evidence to indict anyone involved in these murders.[134]

The very thought of prosecuting a crime that occurred before I was born made my head spin. But the more I learned about the case, the more intrigued I became about the possibility of trying it. Surely, prosecuting such a historically significant case would have been the highlight of my legal career. But what the FBI agent told me next was not encouraging. Even after 50 years, there were still no solid leads on

---

[134] See fn. 3 for the titles of two books written about the Moore's Ford case.

any suspects. And if any suspects were ever identified, they would likely be in their late 70s or 80s – or more likely, dead.

In the years that followed, I was given periodic updates regarding the status of the investigation. Unfortunately, the renewed investigation was never able to uncover anything more than rumors and speculation. Even with the assistance of the Georgia Bureau of Investigation, FBI investigators hit dead end after dead end. And to this day, there is still no answer to the question: Whodunit?

The Randy Peters Case

Randy Peters met and married Linda at a young age. The couple had twin daughters, bought a modest house outside the City of Monroe in Walton County, and started a produce delivery business. When the girls got older, they became active in youth softball and their mother, Linda, was one of their coaches. Their other coach was a married man named Jeff Sargent who also had a daughter on the team. Before long, Linda and Jeff began a lurid extramarital affair that would eventually lead to Randy's murder.

When Randy caught wind of Linda and Sargent's adulterous trysts, he tried to save his marriage, but Linda insisted that she wanted a divorce. Randy told Linda in no uncertain terms, however, that if she tried to divorce him, he would seek custody of the girls. This threat allegedly motivated Linda – in collaboration with persons who are still unknown to this day – to devise a plan to kill Randy, retain custody of the twins, collect on his life insurance policy, and take over sole control of the family's produce business.

On the night that Randy was killed, Linda and the girls left home after dinner for softball practice on the other side of town. After practice, as she would frequently do, Linda dropped the girls off at Randy's parents' house to spend the night.[135] But when Linda arrived home, she told Randy that she had forgotten her softball cleats and needed to return to the softball fields to retrieve them. When Linda returned home a second time, she claimed that she heard Randy exclaim, "I'm shot, I'm shot" as she entered the house. And upon seeing a "shadowy figure" in a central hallway, she ran back to her car and drove away.

Did she drive to the Monroe Police Department to report this crime in progress? No. Did she drive to Randy's parents' house? No. Instead, she drove past these locations to a daycare center parking lot across town where she rendezvoused with her lover Jeff Sargent. Only *after* this meeting did she drive to Randy's parents' house to report what she had allegedly heard and seen. Once there, Linda told Randy's father, "You need to go check on Randy, something's wrong at the house." While Randy's mother called the police, Randy's father drove to his son's house where he discovered Randy's lifeless body lying in a hallway. He had been shot twice at close range with a shotgun.[136]

When police arrived at Randy's house that night, they observed that drawers in the living room and master bedroom had been haphazardly pulled out and dumped, but nothing appeared to have been taken. And curiously, none of Linda's jewelry had been taken. But most strikingly, none of Randy's numerous firearms in a glass display case had been taken. This, the investigators concluded, was not a burglary. They concluded instead that whoever had entered the Peters' house that night was not there to steal, they were there to kill Randy Peters. But why? Who would want Randy dead?

---

[135] This was the Peters' normal routine which allowed Randy and Linda to get up early the next morning and drive to the farmer's market without having to leave their girls at home alone.

[136] Randy's clothing was wet. Investigators later concluded that he had been forced into a hallway bathroom and shot twice at close range in the bathtub. And then, Randy apparently stumbled into the hallway where he collapsed.

Before long, investigators would have a possible answer to this question when they learned about Linda's affair with Jeff Sargent – something that Linda had not mentioned when she was initially questioned by police. And even more suspicious, she failed to mention anything about her clandestine meeting with Sargent that night at the daycare center parking lot. Investigators didn't learn about that until after they questioned Sargent. Moreover, even after Linda admitted that this meeting had taken place, she was never able to give a satisfactory explanation for the purpose or timing of this mysterious tête-à-tête. Thus, investigators came to view Linda as their prime suspect.

The investigators' working theory was that Linda, probably with the knowledge and support of Jeff Sargent,[137] had paid or persuaded someone to kill Randy on her (their) behalf. The killer or killers may have been professional hitmen or they may have been one or more of Linda's sympathetic family members. Investigators speculated that Linda's late-night trip to retrieve her cleats was a ruse – a pre-planned signal to the hitmen who were waiting in the woods behind the home that the "coast was clear." This theory was partly corroborated the next morning when police discovered two distinct sets of footprints leading from the woods to the house. The hitmen theory was further corroborated by the fact that Randy's truck had been taken from the house that night *after* the killing and found abandoned 20 miles away. Investigators determined that neither Linda nor Sargent could have driven it there and gotten back to Monroe.

As far-fetched as the hitman theory might sound, investigators had reason to believe that Linda had access to a considerable sum of money with which to hire a hitman. It turns out that Linda kept the books for the family's produce business and had been secretly squirreling

---

[137] Before lawyering-up, Sargent had told police that if he told them what he knew, he'd get "life or the electric chair."

away a sizable amount of cash in anticipation of her impending divorce. And it was also possible that the hitmen may have been willing to wait for Linda to collect on Randy's life insurance policy. Moreover, as we saw in Chapter 4, finding a hitman in Walton County was not beyond the realm of possibility.

But investigators and I were faced with a dilemma. We had strong circumstantial evidence pointing to Linda as the architect of the plot to kill her husband. But we never recovered the murder weapon, and we had no clue as to the identity of the person or persons who fired the fatal shots. There was arguably enough evidence to establish probable cause to justify an arrest. And likely enough evidence to get an indictment. But I feared that the evidence amassed up to that point would not be enough to secure a conviction.[138] I believed that we needed more conclusive proof, and I thought that the best way to get it was to offer Jeff Sargent immunity in return for his testimony against Linda.[139] What happened next made the national news.

On the day before the hearing on my motion to grant Jeff Sargent immunity, he and Linda got married.[140]

Although Judge Ott subsequently granted my motion to immunize Sargent's testimony against self-incrimination concerns, Sargent's marriage to Linda arguably provided him with the right to invoke Georgia's "spousal testimonial privilege." This long-standing Georgia evidentiary privilege was designed to promote marital harmony by authorizing a person to refuse to testify in a criminal case against his

---

[138] Probable cause is a far cry from proof "beyond a reasonable doubt."

[139] A grant of so-called "use and derivative use immunity" to a witness enables the witness to testify against others without fear that his testimony or any evidence derived therefrom could be used against him in a subsequent prosecution. It thus prevents the immunized witness from refusing to testify against others on 5th Amendment self-incrimination grounds.

[140] Jeff Sargent had divorced his wife shortly before Randy Peters' murder.

or her spouse. But wait a minute! Given the timing of this marriage, wasn't it patently obvious that Linda and Sargent had only gotten married in order to stymie the investigation into the murder of Linda's first, now dead husband![141] How was invoking this testimonial privilege in this case *promoting* marital harmony? Would the law really recognize what I later referred to in my court filings as a "sham marriage?"

Predictably, when I subpoenaed Sargent to appear before the grand jury, his attorney filed a motion to quash the subpoena citing Sargent's spousal testimonial privilege. When Judge Ott reluctantly granted Sargent's motion to quash, I appealed his ruling to the Georgia Court of Appeals. At the oral argument, the three-judge panel seemed extremely supportive of my argument that Sargent's invocation of the spousal testimonial privilege was inconsistent with the legislative purpose for which it had been enacted. Nonetheless, the Court later ruled in a 3-0 opinion[142] that the applicable statutory language was clear and unambiguous – and blanket in its coverage – and that only the legislature could cure this anomalous result.[143]

Now what?

I was still of the opinion that more proof was needed to convict Linda of this crime. I feared that if I attempted to try her with what we had, there was a strong possibility that she would be acquitted. And if acquitted, the principle of Double Jeopardy would have forever barred a retrial – *even if* conclusive proof of Linda's guilt surfaced years later. So, I made the gut-wrenching decision to wait. I was banking on two

---

[141] Prior to the marriage, Linda allegedly told her daughters that, after consulting with her lawyer, she "had to" marry Sargent to prevent him from testifying against her.

[142] State v. Peters, 213 Ga. App. 352 (1994).

[143] Despite attempts to persuade the General Assembly to amend the marital testimonial privilege statute to prevent a person like Sargent from invoking this privilege for crimes occurring prior to a witness' marriage to a suspect, the law remains unchanged. See O.C.G.A. §24-5-503.

possibilities: (1) Sargent and Linda's marriage would fall apart and he would either divorce her (and thereby lose any claim to the spousal testimonial privilege) or agree to testify against her, or (2) someone would tip off police to the identity of the hitmen who would agree to testify against Linda (and Sargent) in return for a lighter sentence.

My decision to hold off on prosecuting Linda (and Sargent) in this case was not a popular one. Randy's parents and the community wanted justice, and they wanted it right then. And I couldn't blame them. Most observers believed that Linda was involved up to her eyeballs in Randy's murder. Yet my decision to delay prosecution allowed her to collect on Randy's life insurance policy and go on with her life. It was so unfair. To this day, my inability to try this case still ranks as one of my biggest disappointments as District Attorney.

But time has a way of healing all wounds, and this one would be healed too – eventually.

In the years that followed, the GBI would occasionally work undercover in an attempt to unearth new evidence in the case. They even drained a lake once looking for the murder weapon. But all of these efforts were to no avail. In 2008, however, this cold case took a dramatic turn. Jeff Sargent suffered a brain aneurism and died.[144] And with Sargent's death, it appeared that the best hope of linking Linda to Randy's murder had died with him. With no realistic expectation of uncovering new evidence, and with little left to lose, perhaps it was time for the State to consider moving forward with Linda's prosecution and giving it their best shot.

---

[144] Sargent's attending physicians apparently did not suspect foul play. But surely the stressful origins and course of this marriage must have contributed, at least in part, to Sargent's premature death.

In 2014, District Attorney Layla Hinton Zon[145] made the decision to seek a murder indictment against the then remarried Linda Peters Sargent Agee.[146] Zon was ably assisted in this prosecution by a former student of mine at UGA Law named Jacqueline Payne Fletcher. Together, they fashioned a strong circumstantial evidence case against Linda. They even asked me to play a small part by testifying as a legal expert on the spousal testimonial privilege in order to explain to the jury the lengths to which Linda had gone to prevent Sargent's testimony against her. And in 2015, twenty-three years after Randy Peter's murder, a Walton County jury answered the whodunit question: They convicted Linda Agee of the murder of Randy Peters, and she was sentenced to life imprisonment.[147]

---

[145] Zon was the last ADA that I had hired prior to my stepping down as District Attorney in 2000.

[146] Following Sargent's death, Linda married for a third time to a man named Agee. When cold case investigators questioned her new husband, he claimed that he had no idea that she had been a suspect in her first husband's death.

[147] NOTE: The Georgia Supreme Court reversed Agee's murder conviction in an opinion dated August 10, 2020. The Court held that the trial court committed harmful error when it permitted the State to introduce Sargent's hearsay statements to police (referenced in fn. 137). Thus, Agee is once again presumed innocent.

CHAPTER 7

Stupid Crimes & Crazy Criminals

Many of the crimes that people commit are just plain stupid. And some of the people who commit these crimes are just plain crazy. As I often told my family, friends, and law students, "you just can't make this stuff up." (Okay. I might not have always used the word "stuff.") Want proof? Read on.

Shortly after becoming District Attorney, we had a run-of-the-mill simple battery case on the arraignment calendar. A young man had gotten into a fight and had kicked and punched another man in front of several witnesses. It was an open-and-shut case and just about as "vanilla" as they come. We offered the young man our standard plea recommendation for a misdemeanor battery: twelve (12) months on probation and a fine of $300 and restitution to the victim.

Well, as it turned out, this young man was a member of a local religious sect – which most of us believed to be more accurately described as a "cult." The young man's mother, who had accompanied her son to court that morning, was not happy with our plea offer. Apparently, the prospect of her son being criminally prosecuted by the "secular authorities" did not sit well with her. Thus, she insisted on speaking with me in my office. At the end of our conversation, I informed her that her son would be treated just like any other mother's son who beat and kicked the crap out of someone in front of a throng of witnesses. At that point, she slowly rose to her feet, stared at me pensively, and said, "Mr. Cook, I will pray that the flesh falls from your bones."

For a few fleeting seconds, I had visions of my staff opening my office door and discovering my skeletonized body slumped over my desk. But after rolling up my shirt sleeve and grasping a portion of my forearm between my thumb and forefinger, I concluded that this woman didn't have as much influence with the Man Upstairs as she thought she did.

A few of my favorite stupid crime and crazy criminal stories appear below.

The "Junk Car" Case

Have you ever seen one of those salvage yards with hundreds of junk cars? Most are located in industrial areas. I had one in my backyard. Well, not literally in my backyard. But it could not have been more than a mile or so away from my house. I would drive by it on my way to work almost every day. And frankly, it didn't really bother me that much. But it was an extreme source of consternation to the adjacent homeowners living in Walnut Grove, Georgia.

The owner-operator of this salvage yard, Buford Rooks[148] had been cited on numerous occasions for violating Walton County's junk car ordinance. On the last such occasion, Mr. Rooks demanded a jury trial, and the case was transferred to Superior Court. To my knowledge, no prosecutor in my Circuit had ever tried a county ordinance violation case. So, I assigned the case to myself.

---

[148] This is not the defendant's real name. I have no problem naming the felons whose crimes I describe in this book, but I'm not inclined to "out" the misdemeanants.

When I met with the surrounding homeowners, they were hopping mad. They told me tales of rats and other vermin that used Rook's junkyard as their base of operation to invade the surrounding neighborhood. They would not be satisfied with a mere fine or even jail time; they wanted the junk cars gone. So, when I met with Mr. Rooks, who chose to act as his own lawyer, my plea offer was simple: remove the 200-300 junk cars from his 8-acre tract within 60 days and I would dismiss the case. Fail to do so and I would recommend 12 months in jail.

Rooks stubbornly drug his feet and when the next trial term arrived, much to Rooks' surprise, I called his case for trial. After the jury was selected, however, Mr. Rooks decided to plead guilty. I had called his bluff, and he folded like a cheap suit. Judge Sorrells sentenced him to 270 days in jail but suspended the sentence on the condition that he remove all of the cars within 45 days. When Rooks thereafter failed to do so, Judge Sorrells tossed him in jail. Rooks was not released until his wife completed the job a few weeks later.

I'll bet that Vincent Bugliosi never successfully tried a junk car ordinance case![149]

The "FUI" Case

Two men were drinking in a rural roadside bar. What could possibly go wrong?

Joe Rutledge, the first man, struck up a conversation with the second man who was sitting next to him. During this conversation, Rutledge learned that the other man was a licensed pilot with a small

---

[149] Bugliosi was the Los Angeles prosecutor who prosecuted Charles Manson for the Tate-LaBianca murders in 1969 and co-authored the best-selling book about the "Manson Family" titled Helter Skelter.

plane parked at the nearby airstrip. "Show me your plane, man," he pleaded. This would not end well.

The two men drove to the airstrip in one of the men's cars. (I'm not sure who drove.) When they arrived, it was pitch dark. But pilots with airplanes registered at the airstrip could "key" the microphone in their planes, and the landing strip lights would illuminate. "Let's taxi the plane on the runway, man," Rutledge pleaded.

As the pilot taxied his Cessna 150 down the runway, Rutledge said, "Let me drive, man." Whereupon the pilot relinquished the controls to the man *without* a pilot's license. And within seconds, the plane was airborne. And within a few more seconds, the plane crashed just 150 feet from the Tall Oaks Apartments. A few more feet and we could have had a real tragedy on our hands. As it was, Rutledge, whose blood-alcohol tested .04%, survived,[150] but the licensed pilot, who tested .13%, did not.

When I was preparing to draft the indictment in this case, I scoured the criminal code for the Homicide by Aircraft statute. To my surprise, there wasn't one! Could it be that no one had ever thought to criminalize flying under the influence? Apparently not. So instead, I was forced to charge Rutledge with involuntary manslaughter premised upon his reckless conduct. Nonetheless, Rutledge was convicted and received a 10-year prison sentence.

After Rutledge's conviction, I persuaded my local legislator to introduce a bill to establish Georgia's first Homicide by Aircraft law. My proposed bill subsequently passed both houses unanimously and was signed by the Governor.[151]

---

[150] The legal limit for operating an aircraft was .04%.

[151] O.C.G.A. §6-2-5.2.

The "Space Shuttle" Case

You have to be pretty desperate to carjack a wrecker truck. Darrin Stinson must have been pretty desperate. He lured a wrecker service driver to a dirt road, robbed him at gunpoint, forced him to strip naked, and stole his wrecker truck. Stinson soon learned, however, that a wrecker truck is not the best choice for a getaway vehicle – they sort of stick out like a sore thumb. So, not surprisingly, Stinson was soon spotted by police, apprehended, and charged with armed robbery and motor vehicle theft.

In the 1990s, the Georgia General Assembly enacted some of the toughest sentencing laws in the country. These so-called "mandatory minimum" statutes were designed to deliver "truth in sentencing."[152] For the offense of armed robbery, for example, the mandatory minimum sentence was ten years in prison. And to ensure that defendants convicted for these offenses would not be prematurely released from prison, the legislature provided that these sentences "shall not be reduced by any form of parole or early release." In other words, a defendant imprisoned for armed robbery had to serve *every day* of his ten-year sentence.

These mandatory minimum statutes were well-received by the law-abiding public and served the public good in several respects. One, they created a powerful deterrent that likely discouraged many would-be felons from attempting to commit such crimes. And two, anyone foolish enough to commit these crimes and unlucky enough to get caught would be kept off the streets for a long, long time. But there was also a downside: Mandatory minimum statutes frequently discouraged defendants from entering into negotiated plea agreements. Few armed robbery defendants, for example, were eager to plead guilty

---

[152] Judges, prosecutors, and the general public had grown tired of seeing defendants who had been sentenced to lengthy prison terms released by the Parole Board after serving just a fraction of their sentences. See O.C.G.A. §17-10-6.1.

to ten years in prison *without* the possibility of parole. So, many of these defendants – even obviously guilty ones – demanded jury trials. I think this explains, in part, why Stinson refused to plead guilty in this case despite overwhelming evidence of his guilt. That and, as you will soon learn, he had more pressing matters to attend to.

When Stinson's trial date arrived, he refused to change out of his jail uniform into more suitable courtroom attire. And he sent word to the judge that he wasn't coming to court. He claimed that he had somewhere else to be. He insisted that he was scheduled to pilot the NASA space shuttle that week. The trial would have to wait. I'm fairly certain, however, that Judge Ott didn't bother to call NASA to check on Stinson's claim before ordering the trial to proceed in Stinson's absence.[153]

Not surprisingly, Stinson was convicted. Following his conviction, Judge Ott pondered whether he could pronounce Stinson's sentence in Stinson's absence. The safest course of action, he concluded, was to have him brought to court – by force if necessary. So, a team of burly deputies was dispatched to bring Stinson to the courtroom. When Stinson arrived, he was shackled at the waist – and was shirtless. When he kicked a chair at this trial attorney John Howell, he was quickly restrained by the aforementioned burly deputies. And when he refused to stop shouting, Judge Ott ordered that he be gagged.[154] When Stinson resisted, the deputies took him to the floor. Judge Ott then stood up, leaned over the bench to get a good look at the prostrate defendant, and pronounced his sentence.

Thankfully, the space shuttle was successfully launched later that week.

---

[153] A defendant may refuse to participate in his own trial. But if he does so, the trial may proceed in his absence. This is known as being tried "in absentia."

[154] The privilege of placing the gag in Stinson's mouth was given to a jailer who Stinson – from inside his jail cell – had doused with a cup of urine days earlier.

The "Columbine Copycat" Case

On April 20, 1999, two, armed, trenchcoat-wearing twelfth-grade students at Columbine High School in Littleton, Colorado, entered their school and murdered twelve of their fellow students and a teacher. At the time, it was the deadliest school shooting in American history. Americans from coast to coast were in shock. And they feared that others might be "inspired" to commit similar "copycat" crimes.[155]

Unfortunately, those fears were soon realized.

Just 8 days after Columbine, a 14-year-old Canadian student entered his school wearing a trench coat concealing a sawed-off shotgun and proceeded to shoot and kill one student. And less than 10 days following the Columbine High School atrocity, an incident occurred in my Circuit. A student at Eastside High School in Newton County named Billy Prince[156] sent emails to students and administrators at several Newton County schools that contained veiled threats to commit a Columbine-like attack on their schools. Prince's emails were written in cryptic, upper and lowercase letters with the subject line reading: "this will break the colorado record" or "Keep an eye on your local schools," and the text of the email reading: "mAy 6, 1999 YoUr ScHoOl iS NeXt."

Parents, students, and administrators were justifiably alarmed. As a result, several schools were closed, and those that chose to remain open were provided with extra, highly visible police protection. The person who sent these emails needed to be found and found quickly. Fortunately, Prince's emails were quickly traced back to his parents' AOL account. And when police came knocking at their door, Prince's

---

[155] Some media reports have suggested that as many as 100 "Columbine-style" school shootings have taken place in the 20 years following the Columbine shootings. https://thehill.com/blogs/blog-briefing-room/news/439263-investigation-shows-more-than-100-copycat-shooters-inspired-by

[156] I have chosen not to use this defendant's real name due to his youth at the time of the crime.

distraught parents fully cooperated and permitted their son to be questioned. When confronted with the threatening emails, Prince readily admitted that he had sent them, but said that it had all just been a prank – that he had no intention of harming anyone. Perhaps, but unlike stealing your high school rival's mascot, this prank wasn't funny; it wasn't funny at all. I knew that we had to send an unmistakably clear message to the community that we weren't going to tolerate such threats – prank or no prank. Thus, I sought and secured a felony indictment against Prince for making terroristic threats.

Prince's attorney, John Strauss, who never gave up without a fight, filed a demurrer to the indictment claiming that it didn't state a crime.[157] He argued that the words "your school is next," rather than being a threat, could have been an innocent, harmless challenge to school rivals, e.g., "when we play your team next, we're going to beat you like we beat that last team we played." I counter-argued that a jury would be entitled to construe Prince's words *in context*, including: (1) his use of upper and lower case letters (like a film noir ransom note) and, (2) mentioning Colorado in the subject line so soon after the Columbine massacre. The Court agreed with me and rejected Prince's demurrer.

Prince eventually pled guilty and was sentenced to a 5-year probated term with the first 4-6 months at a diversion center.

The Joseph Bridges "Escape" Case[158]

It is common for county jail inmates to be transferred from one county jail to another when they have pending charges in more than one jurisdiction. In accordance with this practice, my office once sought to "borrow" a Douglas County inmate named Joseph Bridges in order to

---

[157] A demurrer challenges the sufficiency of the pleadings, i.e., the indictment or accusation, and claims that the defendant can admit its allegations and still be guilty of no crime whatsoever.

[158] Bridges v. State, 256 Ga. App. 355 (2002).

resolve a pending misdemeanor charge against him in Newton County. At the time, Bridges was in the Douglas County jail awaiting transfer to a state prison facility. He had only recently been convicted for a burglary in Douglas County and had been sentenced to serve eight years in prison.

When Bridges arrived at the Newton County jail, he was held until his court date at which he entered a plea of not guilty to the Newton County charge. Whereupon, he was transported from the courthouse back to the Newton County jail. And that's when this routine inmate transfer process went astray. A Newton County jailer apparently didn't see the Douglas County "hold" on Bridges and mistakenly permitted him to post bond on the Newton County misdemeanor charge. Thus, after completing the bond paperwork, Bridges was permitted to walk out of the jail a free man.

Did Bridges attempt to correct the jailer's mistake? Did he say, for example, "Excuse me, Officer, but I do believe that you have made a mistake in authorizing my release. Shouldn't I be transferred back to the Douglas County jail to begin serving my eight-year prison sentence?" Uh, no. He did not say this.

I did not become aware of this snafu until a few days later when I received a phone call from a rather irate Douglas County DA. "What kind of bush league, backwoods operation do you have over there," he inquired? He explained to me that he had personally prosecuted Bridges and that it had been a very hard-fought victory. (If I recall correctly, the burglary victim in that case was a Douglas County Superior Court judge!) After profusely apologizing, I promised him that upon Bridges' capture, I would personally prosecute him for the offense of escape.

But did Bridges really commit the crime of escape? After all, the jailer told him that he was free to go after posting the misdemeanor bond. When I examined Georgia's escape statute, I discovered that it didn't even define the word "escape." Instead, it merely stated that "[a] person commits the offense of escape when he, having been convicted of a felony, intentionally escapes from lawful custody or from any place of lawful confinement."[159] (I thought to myself: "Isn't that like saying that a person commits the offense of "murder" when he *murders* someone?") This legal conundrum would likely come down to proving that Bridges had acted with criminal intent – that he "intentionally escape[d]." Of course, this question was purely academic until Bridges was apprehended.

Bridges' intent to evade his Douglas County prison sentence soon became abundantly clear, however, when his Newton County bail bondsman discovered that Bridges had given him a false address. Thereafter, the Metro Fugitive Squad searched for him for 16 months before finding him eating dinner at a suburban Waffle House. He had been living in a motel across the street from the Waffle House where he was registered under a false name. Not exactly the conduct of someone who was unaware of the wrongfulness of his act in walking out of the Newton County jail while under a pending prison sentence.

When Bridges declined my plea offer to tack on a few extra years to his Douglas County burglary conviction, I kept my promise to the Douglas DA and tried Bridges myself. The jury convicted him and the Court of Appeals affirmed finding that Bridges' post-release conduct clearly evidenced his intent to "escape" from lawful confinement. In so doing, the Court ruled that in the absence of a statutory definition of "escape," the jury was entitled to apply the Webster's Dictionary definition of that word.

---

[159] O.C.G.A. §16-10-52.

CHAPTER 8

Ridiculous!

Being a prosecutor is serious business. Prosecutors must deal with some of society's most intractable problems: child abuse, domestic violence, drug trafficking, gangs, etc. But perhaps more often, we find ourselves handling the mundane and, on occasion, the ridiculous. You might imagine that such cases would be a welcome relief from the stress and strain of prosecuting child molesters, batterers, drug pushers, and gangbangers. But you'd be wrong. Instead, these cases can be infuriating. They tie up a prosecutor's valuable time and resources that could be more productively spent elsewhere. And the cause? It is often due to the pretentiousness of defense attorneys or their stubborn clients – more often the latter. But the worst offenders by far are pro se defendants[160] who insist upon "their day in court."

The cases below represent some of the more ridiculous cases that I prosecuted.

The "Junkman Preacher" Speeding Cases

That's right. I said "cases" – plural. So, you might be wondering, why did I try these speeding cases? Well, although the vast majority of my jury trials involved felonies, as a new ADA, I was permitted to "cut

---

[160] "Pro se" means to represent oneself without the assistance of an attorney.

my teeth" on a few misdemeanors first – including traffic cases. The stakes were low in these cases, and they enabled me to gain valuable trial experience that assisted me in handling more consequential cases in the years that followed.

So, the fifth trial of my fledgling prosecution career in 1988 involved a speeding case. The defendant, Rev. Ezekiel Golden,[161] was a part-time preacher and full-time junk dealer – a real-life Fred Sanford. Earlier that same trial week, I had tried another speeding case involving a very popular local physician who still made house calls. The jury acquitted the good doctor or perhaps more accurately, forgave him, as he had been out making house calls when he was pulled over. When I called the Golden case after having unsuccessfully tried the doctor's case, Judge Greeley Ellis commented, "What is this, the Walton County traffic court?"[162]

Rev. Golden was a rather cantankerous man and insisted on representing himself. I only presented one witness, an experienced Georgia State Patrol officer who had captured the speed of Golden's truck on his hand-held radar gun. To lay the foundation for the admissibility of the radar gun's speed estimate, I was required to walk the Trooper through a series of questions to verify the accuracy of the speed gun and the Trooper's training and certification to operate it. When I was done, it was Golden's turn to cross-examine the Trooper.

Golden approached the witness stand, reached into his pocket, and removed a handful of quarters. He then painstakingly stacked these quarters on the railing in front of the Trooper and asked, "How fast are those coins moving?" Perplexed, the Trooper responded, "Rev.

---

[161] See fn. 148.

[162] Both of these cases would have been handled in a lower court had the defendants not insisted upon a jury trial – available only in Superior Court. These cases were likely called for trial because all of the felony cases on the trial calendar had either pled out or were continued.

Golden, those coins are stationery; they aren't moving at all." At which point Golden triumphantly declared, "Wrong! The Earth is spinning on its axis. Those coins are moving!" That was it; that was Golden's defense. A real head-scratcher. It didn't work. Golden was convicted, sentenced to 10 days in jail, and fined $1000.

Eight years later, I tried my 79th career jury trial. The defendant? You guessed it. The Rev. Ezekiel Golden. The charge? Speeding. Again. This time around, Rev. Golden also had numerous other charges pending (including multiple citations for violating Walton County's junk ordinances). And like the first trial, this trial also culminated in a guilty verdict. But this time, the judge sentenced Rev. Golden to 30 days in jail. Stubbornness has a price.

Ridiculous!

The "Kangaroo Court" Speeding Case

Between Golden No. 1 and Golden No. 2, I tried another speeding case – the Buster Waldrop[163] case.

Okay, by now you are probably wondering why I, the elected District Attorney of the Alcovy Judicial Circuit, was still trying speeding cases. Well, we had a tremendous backlog of cases during my decade in office.[164] And when speeders insisted on "their day in court," it prevented us from trying more serious cases. And that got my boxers in a bunch. So, I occasionally volunteered to try these cases myself to make a point.

---

[163] See fn. 148.

[164] I inherited a huge backlog of cases when I first took office. This backlog was caused, in part, by a federal lawsuit that had held up the appointment of a judge in our Circuit to replace Judge Ellis who had resigned to run for governor. So, for almost a year and one half, we only had one Superior Court judge to handle criminal cases in both counties.

Buster Waldrop was one of these "I want my day in court" guys. And, like Rev. Golden, he insisted on representing himself pro se. On the day of his trial, this Perry Mason wannabe brought a large portfolio with him which contained numerous charts and graphs including an aerial map of the roadway where he had been stopped for speeding. And he had copies of all of the tickets written by the officer who had issued his citation.

Waldrop was about as prepared as a non-lawyer could be. But he had one very big problem. He didn't understand the rules of evidence. So, when he attempted to introduce the exhibits that he had brought to court, I objected to each one, "No foundation, hearsay, irrelevant, etc." Waldrop was clearly frustrated when Judge Sorrells sustained each of my objections. He might as well have left his portfolio at home. The jury quickly convicted him. And Judge Sorrells, noting that Waldrop had an extensive history of traffic law violations, sentenced him to 6 weekends in jail.

Not long after his conviction, Waldrop submitted a Letter to the Editor to the local newspaper accusing Judge Sorrells and me of running a "Kangaroo Court." So incensed was he, that he even attempted to appeal his speeding conviction to the Georgia Court of Appeals. But once again, his lack of legal acumen rendered him hoisted on his own petard – his appeal was summarily dismissed because he had missed the filing deadline. Feeling somewhat vindicated, I sent Judge Sorrells a copy of the Court of Appeals' dismissal Order and appended the following language thereto: "The kangaroos may commence their celebration instanter!"

* * *

As luck would have it, Mr. Waldrop and I would meet again in the same courtroom a few years later when he was summoned for jury duty. You can probably imagine my angst when I saw him sitting in the courtroom. There was no way I could put him on one of my juries. So, when his name was called, I asked the judge if we could approach the bench. I told the judge that based upon our prior courtroom skirmish, I didn't think that Mr. Waldrop could serve as a fair and impartial juror. Mr. Waldrop nodded in agreement. And he was thus excused for cause.

Ridiculous!

The "Septic Tank Sovereign" Case

If you prosecute long enough, you will eventually cross paths with adherents of the so-called "Sovereign Citizen Movement." These folks don't believe that state laws apply to them because, well, they are *sovereign* over themselves and bound only by the common law. If they bother to come to court at all, they will challenge the jurisdiction of the court, refuse to sign any paperwork, and share their unconventional ideology with anyone willing to listen.

The most entertaining sovereign citizen that I encountered was a man named Cletis Hoyer.[165] Hoyer owned and operated a septic tank pumping business. Because he didn't recognize the legitimacy of state and local governments, he refused to secure a business license. Cited numerous times for his failure to do so, he eventually found himself charged in Superior Court.

On his arraignment day, Hoyer arrived in court dressed in his very best overalls and sporting a long beard that extended mid-chest. When I called the calendar, I asked Mr. Hoyer if he had an attorney. "No," he said, but he had brought his "constitutional consultant" with him. Looking to his right, I noticed a man who was dressed almost identically to Hoyer exhibiting an almost identical beard. (Channeling

---

[165] See fn. 148.

their inner ZZ Top, I thought to myself? Or perhaps the Smith Bros. famed for their cough drops?) I cautioned Hoyer's "constitutional consultant" that there were laws against practicing law without a license. I suggested, therefore, that it would be unwise for him to step in front of the bar of the court separating the gallery from the counsel tables.

After many subsequent court appearances, Hoyer grew tired of missing work and allowed himself to be found guilty and fined.

Ridiculous!

The "Roach Coach Robbery" Case

If you've ever been to a large manufacturing facility, chances are you are familiar with the term "roach coach." Busy employees at such job sites rarely have time to go out to eat lunch, so they frequently flock to food trucks in the parking lot to satisfy their hunger. For a "small" processing fee, the operator of one such truck in Covington also cashed the employees' checks. Thus, the roach coach operator needed to keep a large amount of cash on hand – a fact that had apparently not gone unnoticed by Arthur Q. Moody and his robbing crew. Moody along with Stanley Anderson and two others seized on this opportunity three days before Christmas on December 22, 1995, and got away with over $16,000 in cash.

Unfortunately for Moody and two of his cohorts, their juvenile getaway car driver agreed to plead guilty and testify against them. At trial, Stanley Anderson proffered an alibi defense. The defense of alibi involves the *impossibility* of the accused's presence at the scene of the crime at the time of its commission. Attempts to establish an alibi are notoriously flawed. Either the defendant cannot account for his whereabouts at the exact time of the crime or he presents an alibi witness whose credibility is, well, dubious at best. Anderson's proffered alibi suffered from both of these defects. To establish his alibi, Anderson called his live-in girlfriend. Her testimony sounded something like this:

Defense Atty:	Where was Stanley on December 22nd, the day of the robbery?
Girlfriend:	He was at home with me all day.
Defense Atty:	Thank you. No further questions.
Cook:	What were you and Stanley doing on December 15th that year?
Girlfriend:	I have no idea.
Cook:	How about December 31st?
Girlfriend:	How am I supposed to remember that?
Cook:	Well, I was just wondering how it is that you have such a keen memory of December 22nd. Can you enlighten us?
Girlfriend:	I don't remember that day in particular, but I know that Stanley was with me that day because he was with me the *entire* month of December. [I could hear one of the jurors scoff and mumble under his breath, "bulls---."]
Cook:	Are you telling this jury that Stanley never left your side during the entire month of December, not even to go to work or to go out and buy cigarettes?
Girlfriend:	That's what I'm saying.
Cook:	If he didn't go to work, how did he support himself?
Girlfriend:	Oh, I support him. [Even Anderson cringed upon hearing this.]
Cook:	No further questions, Your Honor.

Needless to say, the jury did not find this alibi witness credible and convicted Stanley along with his co-defendants.

Ridiculous!

The "Burglar in the Closet" Case

Harvey Lee Taylor was a notorious Walton County burglar and thief. By the time I tried him for burglary in 1992, he had already been convicted of burglary twice. In this case, he was caught hiding in a bedroom closet at the burglary scene by a Walton County deputy. And a search of Taylor's person incident to his arrest revealed that he had the victim's jewelry in his pocket!

"What were you doing in this house," an investigator asked Taylor following his arrest? "I was walking in the neighborhood and saw a police car. I'm afraid of police, so I went into this house and hid in a closet," Taylor explained. Unfortunately for Taylor, he had no explanation for the investigator's next question: "Why was the home-owner's jewelry in your pocket?"

It took the jury 10 minutes to return a guilty verdict. (Some of the jurors must have had to go to the bathroom before taking a vote.)

Ridiculous!

The "You'll Catch Him Next Time" Case

Rodney Benton was a well-known drug dealer in Covington. But he had an uncanny knack for evading arrest and successful prosecution. On one occasion, a Covington PD officer, Philip Bradford, arrested Benton, cuffed him behind his back, and discovered a rock of crack cocaine in a plastic baggie in his front pocket. Officer Bradford then placed this baggie on the hood of his patrol car while he searched Benton's back pockets. As he did so, Benton bent over and ate the crack rock – baggie and all! Not to be deterred, Officer Bradford transported Benton to the hospital to await the "reappearance" of the contraband. When it didn't "reappear" as quickly as anticipated, Benton was released without being charged.

On another occasion, the local drug task force made a hand-to-hand cocaine buy from Benton. The undercover agent – a very good agent – made a positive identification of Benton as the seller. Unfortunately, the seller's face did not appear clearly on the undercover video of the sale. After about an hour of deliberations, the jury returned a verdict of not guilty.

I was troubled by this verdict because I felt that the agent was extremely credible and that his identification of Benton was solid – with or without video proof. So, following the release of the jury, I asked the foreperson if he would be willing to talk with me about the jury's decision.[166] He gladly offered to do so. But what he told me made me wish I hadn't asked. The foreperson advised me that as soon as the jury had assembled in the jury room following the closing arguments, he called for a preliminary vote. The tally: 12-0 for *guilty*.

W...w...what!, I thought to myself. "How on Earth did you go from 12-0 for guilty to 12-0 for not guilty," I asked incredulously. To which the foreperson replied, "It didn't feel right for us to return a guilty verdict so quickly. And the more we thought about it, the more convinced we became that if Benton was truly a drug dealer, he would be caught again." Really, I thought to myself? What about *this* time!?

Ridiculous![167]

---

[166] I never publicly criticized a jury's verdict – even if I didn't agree with it. Being a juror is not an easy job.

[167] See Chapter 13 – The Thin Blue Line, for the rest of the Benton story.

CHAPTER 9

Politically-Sensitive Cases

District attorneys in Georgia are elected constitutional officers. But unfortunately, unlike judicial races, in district attorney races in Georgia, candidates must declare a political party – Democrat, Republican, or Independent. This never made any sense to me. Like judges, district attorneys should be expected to follow and enforce the rule of law without regard to political considerations. Requiring district attorneys to declare a political party affiliation, on the other hand, leaves them open to claims of partisanship.

When I was a member of the District Attorney's Association of Georgia from 1990-2000, we had several serious discussions about seeking legislation to make the office of District Attorney a non-partisan position. But we were told that the Speaker of the House, Tom Murphy, a powerful Democrat, would never let such a measure make it to the floor for a vote. Moreover, there was opposition to this proposal from within our own ranks from several firmly entrenched Democrat *and* Republican district attorneys.

So, as I mentioned in Chapter 1, when I sought re-election in 1992 and 1996, I was forced to declare a political party affiliation. Despite having to run under a political party banner in those two elections, however, I chose to use the following campaign slogan in each:

"I'm a professional prosecutor, not a politician." By doing so, I wanted to send a clear message to the voters in my Circuit that my prosecutorial decisions would not be dictated by partisan political considerations.

The cases described below illustrate why district attorneys should be free to exercise their prosecutorial discretion without regard to partisan political considerations.

The Jacquelyn Hillman "Criminal Abortion" Case[168]

One of the most heart-breaking cases that I handled as a prosecutor involved a baby boy who was just 1 month shy of full term when he was shot *in utero* – by his own mother. He died. She lived. And I chose to prosecute her.

The pregnant woman in this tragic case was just 18 years old and already had one child whose father was not in the picture. When she became pregnant again by another man who, like the first man, wasn't interested in marriage or fatherhood, she apparently became depressed. One day, she carried a loaded pistol with her to the bathroom, sat in the tub, placed the barrel of the gun against *her abdomen*, and pulled the trigger. The baby boy was struck by the bullet and was pronounced dead on arrival at the hospital. The young woman survived.

After reading the investigative file – including the child's autopsy report, I reached the conclusion that the pregnant woman's intent was to kill her unborn child. Why else would she point the gun at her abdomen? If her intent had been to commit suicide, she could have (1) waited and killed herself *after* delivering the child, or (2) given her unborn child a chance of survival by pointing the gun at her head or chest. Surely, therefore, her conduct could not be excused. It was criminal.

---

[168] Hillman v. State, 232 Ga. App. 741 (1998).

But what could I charge this young woman with? My first thought was the crime of "feticide." But Georgia's feticide statute didn't fit these facts. The crime of feticide required that the killer be someone *other than* the mother of the fetus, i.e., a third person.[169] The only other criminal statute that arguably applied to these facts was Georgia's criminal abortion statute.[170] I knew, however, that if I charged her with criminal abortion, I would be walking headlong into a firestorm. But I had no choice. The criminality of this woman's actions had to be addressed; this child's life had to be worth something. Moreover, punishment aside, this young woman and her surviving child needed help – the kind of help that court-supervised probation could provide. So, I put on my asbestos suit and secured an indictment.

Well, as you can imagine, local, state, and national "support groups" immediately came to the young woman's defense. How dare I prosecute this poor distraught woman!? The fact that my plea offer to Hillman included mental health counseling and asked for absolutely *no jail time* did not seem to placate the support groups. Why not? In my opinion, these support groups were not truly concerned about this young woman or her surviving child – and they apparently had no concern whatsoever for the deceased child. They were only concerned with one thing: The State's attempt to interfere with a woman's right to terminate her pregnancy. To them, it was all about abortion.

Following her indictment, Hillman filed a motion to quash[171] claiming that her actions did not constitute a crime under Georgia's abortion statute. She claimed that only a doctor performing an illegal abortion, not the pregnant woman upon whom it was performed,

---

[169] See O.C.G.A. 16-5-80.

[170] See O.C.G.A. 16-12-140.

[171] See fn. 157 (defining demurrers).

could be charged. Although Judge Ott denied the demurrer to the indictment, he granted the defendant's request for an interlocutory appeal. And following oral arguments, a three-judge panel of the Georgia Court of Appeals agreed with Hillman's interpretation of Georgia law. They held that a pregnant woman could not be prosecuted under Georgia's criminal abortion law – even if it was she, rather than a doctor, who directly performed the act aborting her child. So, according to the Court of Appeal's decision, Hillman's act was *legal* under Georgia law.

My primary job as a prosecutor was to enforce the law and to seek justice. This outcome didn't seem like justice to me. Hillman would go unprosecuted. She and her living child would receive no court-ordered support services. And there was absolutely nothing standing in her way (or, for that matter, anyone else's) of doing the same thing in the future. So, I asked my state senator to sponsor an amendment to the feticide statute that would make it a crime for a pregnant woman to perform an act with intent to kill her viable fetus. The Senator and I both testified before the Senate Judiciary Committee in support of our amendment. But again, the "support groups" were out in force. We were outnumbered tenfold.

When I was leaving the State Capital that day, WSB TV reporter Sally Sears stopped me and asked me why I was so passionate about this issue. To answer her question, I reached into my coat pocket, retrieved an autopsy photograph of Hillman's dead baby boy with a gaping bullet hole in its abdomen, and showed it to her. "That's why," I said.

Unfortunately, the support groups are a powerful lobby. The proposed legislation never made it out of the Judiciary Committee.

The Voter Fraud Case

What are the odds that 101 of 106 absentee ballots from four voting precincts would be cast for the same primary candidate? Would your opinion change if I told you that the voting precincts consisted primarily of housing project residents – the majority of whom were black? What if I told you that *all* of these votes were cast in the *Republican Primary?*

When I was alerted to these figures by the losing candidate in the Republican Primary, I was immediately suspicious that voter fraud had occurred.[172] My political science background told me that it was a statistical aberration for a candidate in a two-person race to receive 95% of the vote. And for a *Republican* candidate in the 1990s to have received so many votes in a Black housing project was well-nigh impossible. So, I directed my Victim's Services Director Joe Rickman to canvas these housing projects to see if he could figure out what had happened.

It turns out that two "get out the vote" campaign workers – who had worked almost exclusively for *Democrat* candidates in the past – had been hired by one of the Republican Primary candidates to generate support for his candidacy in the Black community. Fair enough. No problem with that. So, what did these two campaign operatives actually do? First, they knocked on doors and persuaded black residents in these housing projects to request absentee ballots. Then, when the absentee ballots arrived, they assisted these voters in filling out the ballots. And finally, they made sure that the completed ballots were mailed back to the Voter Registration Office. This fraudulent scheme is sometimes referred to as "ballot harvesting."

---

[172] This statistical aberration may have accounted for the margin of victory in that primary. The victorious candidate won by a margin of only 74 votes – 1596 to 1522. The losing primary candidate could have filed an appeal to the State Board of Elections, but chose not to do so.

The fraudulent nature of this scheme became crystal clear when these voters were called to give testimony before the grand jury. The stories they told were, to say the least, disheartening. They testified that these two campaign workers, unbeknownst to them, had requested *Republican* Primary ballots and then, upon the arrival of the ballots, told them who to vote for – and likely filled out many of the ballots themselves.[173] I'll never forget the response of one elderly woman who I asked, "Did you know that you had voted for a Republican candidate?" Astonished, she replied, "What? I'm 80 years old and I've never done that before in my life!"[174] Both of these defendants later pled guilty and were banned from participating in "get out the vote" operations while on probation.

You might think that I would have been lauded for enforcing the state's election laws and for seeking to safeguard the integrity of our state's elections. You would be wrong. I was attacked from both sides. The Democrats on the County Commission resented me for prosecuting their long time "get out the vote" campaign workers (and for exposing their "ballot harvesting" scheme). And the Republicans on the County Commission were angry with me for generating so much bad publicity for the "winning" Republican Primary candidate. So, in a truly bipartisan move, the Democrat *and* Republican County Commissioners voted to slash my office's budget for equipment and supplies the following year by more than $20,000![175]

---

[173] NOTE: There was never any evidence to suggest that the candidate himself had encouraged his workers' unlawful behavior.

[174] There is no doubt in my mind that similar voter fraud schemes had benefitted Democrat candidates in Newton County for many years prior to this incident.

[175] Although district attorneys are state-paid constitutional officers, they depend upon the county commissions in their Circuits to fund the operations of their offices – including the provision of office space, support staff, and supplies.

By exposing voting irregularities that were ostensibly condoned by *both* political parties in Newton County, I had crossed an imaginary political boundary line. And as a result, I was taught a hard lesson about politics: While it may take a "professional prosecutor" to fairly and impartially enforce the rule of law, it takes a *politician* to keep the Xerox machine stocked with toner and copy paper.

This disillusioning episode of political retribution contributed greatly to my decision not to run for a 4th term in office.[176]

The "Do the Right Thing" Case

Most criminal cases that survive pretrial screening procedures – preliminary hearings, grand jury, and the exercise of prosecutorial discretion – are resolved by a negotiated plea of guilty, rather than a trial.[177] As you probably know, these negotiated guilty pleas are the result of plea bargaining – a process in which a prosecutor and a defense attorney attempt to reach a mutually agreeable sentencing recommendation. What most people don't know, however, is that judges are not required to accept such plea agreements. Although relatively rare, judges sometimes reject plea agreements when they believe that the recommended sentence is either too lenient or too harsh.

In my experience, when a judge rejected a plea agreement, his or her objection to the recommended sentence was often premised on a less-than-full understanding of the facts and strength of the evidence. For whereas a prosecutor and defense attorney may study a defendant's case for many weeks or months before reaching a negotiated plea agreement, the judge presiding over the defendant's guilty plea at the

---

[176] See Chapter 1.

[177] Recent studies suggest that only about 3% of criminal cases are resolved by trials. Thus, approximately 97% are plea-bargained. https://www.nacdl.org/Document/TrialPenaltySixthAmendmentRighttoTrialNearExtinct

arraignment may only hear a 5-minute recitation of the facts. Thus, unlike the parties to a negotiated plea agreement, a judge usually only hears the *CliffsNotes* version of the case. To a certain extent, this was an unavoidable consequence of crowded criminal arraignment calendars that sometimes numbered well in excess of 75 cases.

I also found that judges tended to reject negotiated plea agreements most often when one of the two following situations were involved: (1) they had a "pet peeve" regarding a certain category of crime and insisted upon an unreasonably harsh sentence in such cases, or (2) they feared a political backlash if, by accepting a seemingly lenient plea agreement, they were to be viewed as "too soft on crime."[178] One of my judges viewed the toppling of a cemetery headstone with particular disdain – an excellent example of the first situation. This was his "pet peeve." Woe to the defendant appearing before this judge charged with that crime. The case described below – which involved the same judge – illustrates the second situation, how a judge's fear of being labeled "soft on crime" can sometimes undermine a prosecutor's attempt to achieve a just result.

Michael Davis[179] accepted a ride to town with three guys from his neighborhood. Unfortunately, the 15-year-old driver fancied himself as a wannabe gang leader. When the driver spotted a vulnerable target in a motel parking lot, he stopped his car, pulled a pistol, and said, "Let's rob that guy." He looked at Davis and said, "You're the lookout." The driver and the two other occupants got out of the car and proceeded to rob the motel guest at gunpoint. Before long, all four young men were arrested and charged with armed robbery. As such, each faced the same penalty: 10 years in prison *without* the possibility of parole.

---

[178] Judges serving in the trial level courts in Georgia must stand for election every four years – hence susceptible to political pressures.

[179] Not his real name.

After Davis' case was indicted, however, I was approached by several law enforcement officers and school administrators who painted a very different picture of this young man. Davis, a high school senior, was a B+ student who was well-liked by schoolteachers and school resources officers. And his attorney, John Strauss, Jr., provided me with additional information about his stable, two-parent home and his excellent prospects of going to and succeeding in college.

Frankly, after hearing all of these people "going to bat" for Davis, I might have dismissed his case outright if he had immediately turned himself and his companions in after the crime. But since he didn't, I offered to let him plead guilty to the lesser-included offense of simple robbery. And instead of 10 years without the possibility of parole, I offered him 90 days at a summer boot camp under the First Offender Act. This disposition would allow him to attend college in the fall. And if he kept his nose clean, the record of his conviction would be erased. He gratefully accepted my offer.

When Strauss and I presented Davis' negotiated plea agreement to the judge, however, the judge rejected it. His reasoning? He didn't want to be seen as undercutting the Legislature's policy of imposing a mandatory minimum 10-year prison sentence in an armed robbery case. Strauss and I were both caught off guard – "stunned" might be a more apt description. Although Davis was permitted to withdraw his guilty plea that day, his entry of a not guilty plea was only a temporary solution.

What to do? I was not about to be a party to sending this young man with a promising future to prison for 10 years. What I decided to do was this: I related the testimonials that I had received about Davis to the same grand jury that had indicted him and asked them if they would be willing to issue an official grand jury recommendation to the judge to accept my plea recommendation. The grand jury agreed and adopted my proposal. And the judge subsequently agreed to accept the original plea agreement.[180] The grand jury's recommendation had given the judge "political cover." In the end, the system worked. It had done the right thing.[181]

---

[180] After this case was resolved, I received a letter from Strauss thanking me for fighting for his client. He wrote, in part: "I merely wanted to thank you for the concern and attention that you have given toward the ends of justice in the [Michael Davis case]."

[181] This case illustrates how prosecutors and defense attorneys frequently work together to achieve a just result.

CHAPTER 10

Death Penalty Cases

In *Furman v. Georgia* (1972), the United States Supreme Court held that the imposition of the death penalty under then-existing state death penalty statutes constituted cruel and unusual punishment under the 8th Amendment. The Court's reasoning was not that the death penalty was unconstitutional per se, but that the then-existing state death penalty statutes failed to adequately guide a jury's sentencing decision resulting in an arbitrary and capricious application of the death penalty. Four years later in *Gregg v. Georgia* (1976), the Court re-authorized the imposition of the death penalty in states that had adopted more narrowly-tailored death penalty statutes. Such statues limited the type of cases in which the death penalty could be sought and provided juries with greater guidance regarding the exercise of their sentencing discretion. Following *Furman* and *Gregg* (and their progeny), the death penalty could only be imposed in murder cases accompanied by so-called "statutory aggravating circumstances,"[182] and then, only after the jury

---

[182] In Georgia, for example, statutory aggravating circumstances include: proof that a murder was committed during the commission of another murder, a rape, an armed robbery, or a kidnapping; or proof that a murder was "outrageously or wantonly vile, horrible, or inhuman in that it involved torture, depravity of mind, or an aggravated battery to the victim." See O.C.G.A. 17-10-30(b).

weighed the aggravating and mitigating circumstances surrounding the crime and the character of the convicted killer.

The death penalty continues to be a highly controversial issue in this country. Polls indicate that the American people are almost evenly split in their views regarding the death penalty - pro and con.[183] As of the writing of this book, twenty-eight (28) states have a death penalty statute on their books. The death penalty is also authorized by federal law for certain federal crimes and by the Uniform Code of Military Justice. Although I respect those who hold religious, moral, or ethical objections to capital punishment, I have always been a supporter of the death penalty in theory, if not in practice. Why? Because I believe that for particularly heinous murders that shock the conscience of the community, the death penalty may be the only sentence that is capable of meeting all of the traditional rationales for sentencing and corrections.

Among these rationales, in no particular order, are the following:

- Punishment – the generally accepted view that the punishment should fit the crime, i.e., the sentence imposed should be proportionate to the crime committed.[184]

- Retribution – the very human desire of the living to avenge the murder of a loved one or a beloved member of one's community.[185]

---

[183] See https://www.pewresearch.org/fact-tank/2018/06/11/ us-support-for-death-penalty-ticks-up-2018/

[184] For example, in my opinion, it would have been extremely unjust for Timothy McVeigh, the bomber of the Murrah Federal Building in Oklahoma City in 1995, to have been given a life sentence instead of the death penalty for killing 168 people and injuring more than 680 others. And if Osama bin Laden had been captured alive....

[185] I met with the family members of many murder victims. You simply can't understand their pain unless you have suffered a similar loss.

- Deterrence – the logical proposition that the prospect of being put to death deters *at least some* would-be killers from committing premeditated murder.

- Incapacitation – the realization that the death penalty is the only way to ensure that a killer won't kill again, because even a life sentence without the possibility of parole will not guarantee the safety of correctional officers and fellow inmates – or the public in the event of an escape.

One of the most difficult and consequential decisions that a district attorney in Georgia must make is whether to seek the death penalty in a murder case. Of the more than 90 homicides in my Circuit during my tenure as District Attorney, I chose to seek the death penalty in five (5) cases involving eight (8) defendants – some of whom were co-defendants. If this number seems small to you, it is probably because my personal criteria for seeking the death penalty were more demanding than that of Georgia's death penalty statute. Why? Because I believed that the death penalty should be reserved for the "worst of the worst."

I describe three of my death penalty cases below.

The Roseberry & Manuel Cases[186]

On a June night in 1997, two men entered Harry's Food Mart, an old-fashioned Ma & Pa convenience store located on the outskirts of the City of Porterdale in Newton County. The taller, stouter man was armed with a sawed-off shotgun. The shorter, thinner man wielded a small-caliber pistol. The two men demanded all of the money in the cash register and the owner, Harry Hodges, obediently handed over

---

[186] Roseberry v. State, 274 Ga. 301 (2001); Manuel v. State, 276 Ga. 676 (2003).

the contents of the drawer. "Turn around," the shorter man said. As Hodges slowly turned his back on the robbers, he was shot execution-style in the back of the head by the shorter man. The two men then fled up the street to a waiting car.

Miraculously, even after having been shot in the head at close range, Hodges remained conscious and was able to dial 911 to summon help. In fact, he was conscious when paramedics arrived and remained so in the ambulance on the trip to Newton General Hospital. When Investigator Ezell Brown[187] met with Hodges in the Emergency Room a short time later, Hodges was able to give him a good description of the two armed robbers before he slipped into a coma. Five days later, Hodges died at an Atlanta trauma center.

Initially, the investigation stalled. But as was my frequent practice in whodunit cases, I asked the GBI to assign an agent to assist. With help of GBI Agent Bobby Stanley, investigators were ultimately able to identify two suspects: Tremayne Roseberry and Robert Manuel. Roseberry, age 23, fit the description of the taller man and was already well known to law enforcement in Newton County. He had prior convictions and had served time. And Manuel, age 19, fit the description of the slender man and already had a record for committing an armed robbery years earlier as a juvenile. The investigation revealed that these two aimless, dope-smoking youths had targeted Harry's Food Mart because, in their words, it was "a good lick." Translation: It was "easy money."

But was this a death penalty case? The decision would be mine to make.[188] The minimum requirements for seeking the death penalty under Georgia's death penalty statute were clearly present: a murder

---

[187] Brown would later become the Sheriff of Newton County.

[188] In Georgia, the elected District Attorney, not the grand jury, makes this decision.

had been committed during the course of an armed robbery. But did this case meet my higher personal standards? Among the additional factors that I typically insisted upon before seeking the death penalty were: (1) the murder victim must be innocent,[189] (2) the perpetrator must either have a violent criminal history or the killing must have been unusually heinous, [190] and (3) the identity of the perpetrator must be clearly established by the evidence.[191]

In my estimation, the Hodges murder case was exactly the kind of case that merited the death penalty. These two men had committed a cold, calculated, and heinous murder of a hard-working citizen in our community. They had already demonstrated by their prior serious brushes with the law that they were incorrigible – and dangerous. And the evidence against each was compelling. Thus, I announced the State's intention to seek the death penalty against both Roseberry and Manuel. Under Georgia law, however, they had the right to be tried separately.

Key evidence in these cases included the testimony of a man who claimed that he had transported Roseberry and Manuel to the vicinity of Harry's Food Mart that night and saw Roseberry get out of his car with a sawed-off shotgun. Another critical piece of evidence connecting Roseberry and Manuel to this crime was Hodge's physical description of his assailants at the Emergency Room. Although Hodges was obviously unavailable to testify at their trials, his so-called "dying

---

[189] Death penalty cases require an extraordinary commitment of time and resources. I did not think it was appropriate to commit the State's limited resources in a case where the murder victim was "up to no good" at the time he was killed, e.g., he was attempting to purchase illegal drugs.

[190] The jury in a death penalty case is instructed that it may consider the defendant's character and future dangerousness when fixing the punishment. Thus, unless a crime is extraordinarily heinous, it is unlikely that a jury will recommend the death penalty for a defendant with no prior (violent) criminal history.

[191] There is no room for error in death penalty cases.

declaration" was ruled admissible as an exception to the general prohibition against hearsay.

In Roseberry's case, I had an important additional piece of evidence. One of Roseberry's cousins inadvertently let slip in the presence of a Covington Police officer that Roseberry had admitted to her that he had participated in the Hodges murder. When I spoke with this witness in my office, however, she was adamant that she wasn't going to testify against Roseberry. I promptly placed a subpoena in her hand and told her that she had no choice in the matter – whereupon she angrily stormed out of my office. So, when she failed to honor her subpoena and appear on the first day of the trial, I secured a "material witness warrant" and had her jailed until it was time for her to testify.[192] Unsurprisingly, when she took the witness stand, she lied and denied having previously spoken of Roseberry's confession. But her denial enabled me, over Roseberry's hearsay objection, to call the Covington Police officer to impeach (discredit) her testimony and to inform the jury of her previous statement made in the officer's presence. Moreover, Roseberry foolishly took the stand at his trial and said that he was near Harry's Food Mart that night, not to rob it, but to sell cocaine![193]

In Manuel's case, I was able to introduce evidence of Manuel's prior juvenile armed robbery as a so-called "similar transaction." In the prior crime, as in the Harry's Food Mart robbery, Manuel had used a small-caliber pistol. This was an important piece of corroborating

---

[192] The judge appointed an attorney to represent Roseberry's cousin and, as I understand it, he advised her to sue me for false arrest. She never did. And I wasn't worried because the law clearly authorized me to seek her arrest in order to secure her attendance at trial when she failed to honor her subpoena.

[193] You may recall my previous statement regarding the dangers inherent in a defendant's decision to waive his 5th Amendment privilege.

evidence to show that it was Manuel, not Roseberry, who possessed the handgun that fired the fatal gunshot.

Ultimately, both Manuel and Roseberry were convicted, but the juries in both cases recommended life imprisonment rather than death.[194] Although jury deliberations are conducted behind closed doors, if I had to guess, I'd say that these juries chose life in Manuel's case because he was just 19 years old at the time of the crime, was of low-average intelligence, and was described as a "follower," and in Roseberry's case, because he wasn't the "triggerman."

If Roseberry had fired the fatal gunshot, I think the jury would have recommended the death penalty in his case. And frankly, even though Roseberry was not the shooter, I thought the case for the death penalty against him was more compelling than the one against Manuel. Between the two, Roseberry was unquestionably the mastermind of this crime. Moreover, I presented a very disturbing piece of aggravating evidence in Roseberry's sentencing phase. Years earlier, while incarcerated at a probation diversion center, he was assigned to pick up roadside trash with an inmate work crew. His fellow inmates testified that on one such occasion, Roseberry found a puppy in the tall grass. They then witnessed Roseberry drop-kick the puppy like a football – killing it.

The Kendra Durden "Highway 138 Murder" Case[195]

Death penalty cases against women in Georgia are so rare that it is not unusual for there to be only one woman on Georgia's death row at any given time – or none.[196] Women simply don't commit violent crimes

---

[194] At the time of their trials, Georgia had not yet adopted the "life without parole" option.

[195] Durden v. State, 274 Ga. 868 (2002).

[196] In 2015, Kelly Gissendaner was executed for orchestrating the murder of her husband in order to collect his life insurance.

at anywhere near the rate of men. And when they do, their crimes seldom involve the kind of "aggravating circumstances" that warrant the death penalty.

The only woman I ever sought the death penalty against was a woman named Kendra Durden. Durden was a young mother who ditched her boyfriend – the child's father – and moved to the City of Sparta in Hancock County where she immediately associated herself with a gang.[197] Before long, she became somewhat of a "queen bee" in the Folks gang. The male gang members vied for her affections and sought to provide for her needs. Durden's most immediate need was for money to rent a trailer home. So, late one Saturday night, Durden and three male gang members drove toward Atlanta looking for someone to rob.

After finding no suitable targets at a Waffle House, they stopped at a 24-hour Kroger's grocery store in Conyers to buy snacks. But when Durden approached the checkout aisle, she found herself in line behind someone who was paying for his groceries with a $100 bill. They had found their "target." The customer was a young man named Patrick Ragan who was on his way home after having just completed his night shift at an Atlanta area business. Upon returning to the car, Durden informed the others about what she had seen and they quickly devised a plan to follow Ragan to his house, rob him, and ransack his home. According to one of the backseat passengers, Durden was "crumpted." Translation: She was excited about what was about to happen.

With Durden driving, the gang members followed Ragan as he drove north on Highway 138. And they drove, and drove, and drove. The increasingly restless gang members had mistakenly assumed that

---

[197] To this day, many law enforcement officers warn others to stay out of Hancock County due to its reputation for lawlessness.

Ragan lived near the 24-hour Kroger's. But he didn't. In fact, he lived a considerable distance away in Walton County. In fact, when they first encountered him in Conyers, he was only about halfway home. Thus, when Ragan left the grocery store parking lot, he still had a long way to go.

With each passing mile, the gang members grew more and more frustrated. And they feared that they would soon run out of gas. That's when the front seat passenger, a young man named Robert Winkfield, directed Durden to speed up and pull alongside Ragan's car. As Durden mashed the gas pedal, Winkfield rolled down the front passenger window and steadied a 9mm pistol on the door frame. And as Durden maneuvered her car closer and closer to Ragan's, she pleaded with Winkfield, "Don't punk out on me now. If you love me, you'll do it for me." When the two cars were side by side, Wingfield aimed his pistol at an unsuspecting Ragan and squeezed off two rounds. Both bullets found their target, one striking Ragan in the neck and the other in his torso, each leaving a large gaping wound. Ragan thereafter lost control of his car. It careened off the road and crashed into a stand of trees – scattering the groceries that he had just purchased across the backseat. Ragan bled out in minutes.[198]

Now what? The gang members had just shot and killed a total stranger. Was there something of value on Ragan's person or in his car worth stealing? They'll never know because they didn't bother to find out. When they observed other cars approaching, they got scared and drove away, leaving behind their scene of carnage. As a result, they got absolutely nothing from their random act of murder. Nothing. Absolutely nothing.

---

[198] In the years that followed, I would drive past this spot on Highway 138 every time that I drove from home to my Walton County office. It was a constant reminder of the consequential nature of my work as a prosecutor.

Was this a death penalty case? As in the Roseberry and Manuel case, this too was a murder committed during the course of an armed robbery. And the heinous nature of the crime was self-evident. I later learned that Ragan was the beloved son of a mother who had recently lost her husband in a car accident. And now, thanks to this group of reprobates, she had lost a son, too. Yeah, this was a death penalty case – *if* police could figure out who had committed this senseless crime. As mentioned in Chapter 6, stranger-on-stranger homicides are among the most difficult crimes to solve. And had it not been for extraordinary police work, these four out-of-town strangers might never have been caught.

To solve this crime, investigators first wanted to know who had last seen the victim alive. This task was aided when they found a time-stamped Kroger's grocery receipt in Ragan's car. To follow this lead, investigators traveled to Conyers to interview the cashier who had rung up Ragan's purchases. The cashier remembered Ragan and was able to give a vague description of the next customer in line. But more importantly, she provided the investigators with a copy of the cash register receipt issued to the next customer in line. This receipt showed that that purchase had been made with an EBT (welfare) card – an EBT card issued to Kendra Durden. Durden and her three male companions were subsequently located and questioned by investigators. Their interlocking statements combined with other corroborating evidence led investigators to charge each with capital murder.

After a thorough investigation, I decided to drop the charges against and grant immunity to the two backseat passengers. Neither one had any significant criminal history, and neither played a significant role in the crime. And both had been very cooperative when questioned by police. It was obvious to me that the two main actors were Durden and Winkfield. I then elected to try Durden first. Why? I truly felt that although Durden had not been the triggerman, she was the "driving force" behind the crime – literally. For had she not accelerated her car to catch up to Ragan's car, he'd likely be alive today. Moreover, it was clear to me that this crime had been committed for her and at her direction. I quickly learned, however, that prosecuting a female defendant in a death penalty case would have unique challenges.

The defense team did everything they could to use Durden's gender to their advantage. For example, when Durden was arrested, her mug shot looked like a Hollywood version of a female gang member – disheveled hair, leather jacket, and gold jewelry. But when she appeared at her jury trial, she more closely resembled the librarian character played by Donna Reed in *It's a Wonderful Life* – you remember, the homely one that would have existed if George Bailey had never been born.

Another gender sympathy play was attempted in the death penalty phase of the trial. In her closing argument, one of the defense attorneys attempted to tearfully describe an incident that had occurred in Judge Ozburn's chambers during a pretrial hearing. This incident, however, had never been, and likely could not have been, introduced during either phase of the trial. Nonetheless, the defense attorney began to describe how Judge Ozburn had kindly offered Durden a Kleenex tissue when he noticed her weeping in his office. I immediately objected. Clearly, this incident was not a "fact in evidence" – thus, it was an inappropriate subject matter for closing argument. Moreover, it was irrelevant, for it spoke to Judge Ozburn's character, *not* Durden's. My objection was sustained.

Although not a gender-based strategy, the defense had proffered a curious defense to the murder charge itself in the guilt/innocence phase of the trial. They claimed that Durden had been "coerced" to participate in this murder by the other gang members in the car. The problem was: Georgia law doesn't recognize the defense of "coercion" in a murder case. Why not? The answer is quite simple: No one has the right to save their own life by taking the life of an *innocent* third person. Here, even if Durden had felt pressured to cooperate (an argument clearly refuted by the evidence in this case), she had no right to assist Winkfield in killing Ragan in order to save her own life.

Durden was convicted, but the jury spared her life.

What to do about Winkfield? Although I still believed that Winkfield was deserving of the death penalty, I didn't think that seeking it would be fair in light of the jury's decision not to impose it against Durden – who, as I opined above, was the more culpable of the two. Thus, I negotiated a plea agreement with Winkfield's attorney that permitted him to plead guilty and receive a life sentence with the condition that he not seek parole for 30 years.[199]

The Brian "Chico" Terrell Case

John Henry Watson was a self-made man. Born in Georgia, he moved to the Midwest, started a family, and established a chain of dry cleaners. When it came time to retire, Watson moved back south and purchased a modest home in Newton County on Highway 142 just outside of the City of Covington. Unfortunately, he suffered a heart attack and had to have bypass surgery. Worse still, he had kidney disease and had to have dialysis three times a week. Nonetheless, at age 70, he still managed to live at home by himself.

One day Watson met a woman named Barbara Terrell – a volunteer at his kidney dialysis center. Despite their age difference – she was

---

[199] Such "plea contracts" are enforceable because both sides are giving up something. (In civil contract law, this is known as "consideration.") I forfeited the State's right to seek the death penalty and Winkfield forfeited the right to seek parole after 14 years – the applicable eligibility date for murder at the time.

much younger than he, they became fast friends. In time, she became increasingly involved in Watson's life. She would occasionally cook, clean, and run errands for him. And her son, Brian Terrell, who went by the nickname Chico, would sometimes cut Watson's grass and do chores around his house.

Unfortunately, Barbara's son Chico was nothing more than a common criminal. He had committed numerous low-level crimes before graduating to – and acting as the ringleader of – an armed robbery in Dekalb County. In that crime, he and several of his running buddies targeted a drug dealer's house, intending to kill everyone in the house and take what they could get. Fortunately, they abandoned their plan to kill the occupants and settled for roughing them up and taking their drugs, money, and a car. Chico and his cohorts, however, were soon arrested and Chico pled guilty to the lesser-included offense of robbery and received a 5-year prison sentence.[200]

In May of 1992, after serving less than half of his prison sentence, Chico was granted parole and returned to Newton County to live with his mother. Although he didn't have a job, his mother soon noticed that he had somehow come into a substantial sum of money – enough to buy a used blue Cadillac automobile and nice clothes. Despite her inquiries, Chico never gave his mother a satisfactory answer regarding the source of his newfound wealth. All he would tell her was: "I'm a grown man, Momma." She suspected, however, that he was selling drugs.

On Saturday, June 20th, the mystery surrounding Chico's sudden influx of cash became clear. When Mr. Watson opened his bank statement that day, he discovered that Chico had stolen and forged a series of his personal checks exceeding $8700. Watson was devastated.

---

[200] If Terrell had been tried in Dekalb County on the original charge of armed robbery, he would have received a mandatory minimum prison sentence without the possibility of parole and would not have been outside prison walls to commit this crime.

How could Barbara's son betray him like that? Later that day, Watson summoned Barbara to his home and showed her the canceled checks. She immediately recognized the handwriting – it was Chico's. She too was devastated. What to do? Watson was conflicted. He didn't want to hurt Barbara, but he couldn't let Chico get away with stealing his money. So, he asked Barbara to relay a message to Chico – an ultimatum: "Pay me back the money you stole from me by Monday or I'll report you to police and seek a warrant for your arrest."

Before Noon on Monday, however, Mr. Watson would be dead.

Watson's ultimatum presented a significant dilemma for Chico. One, as he told his mother on several occasions that weekend, he didn't have any money to pay Watson back – he had spent all of Watson's money on the Cadillac and the fancy clothes. Two, he had been warned by his parole officer that if he was arrested for any new felony offense while on parole – like forgery – his parole would be revoked, and he would be returned to prison to complete his Dekalb County robbery sentence.

Chico had no intention of going back to prison.

On Sunday night, June 21st, Chico and his younger cousin Jermaine Johnson spent the night at a motel within a mile of Watson's house. Upon checking in, they accidentally locked the car keys to Chico's blue Cadillac in the car. Thus, when the two men got up early the next morning, they had to break one of the car's rear passenger windows to retrieve the car keys. Once having done so, Chico instructed Johnson to drive him to Watson's house, drop him off at the street, and return to pick him up at 9:00am.[201] As Chico exited the car, Johnson

---

[201] Chico knew that Watson would be leaving his house at around that time because he knew that Watson received his kidney dialysis treatments at 9:00am on Mondays, Wednesdays, and Fridays.

observed a .38 revolver in Chico's hand. Johnson then returned to the motel, set a wake-up alarm, and took a nap.

Shortly before 9:00am, as Watson emerged from his house to drive himself to the dialysis center, Chico was at the corner of the garage waiting to ambush him. And before Watson could get to the truck that he had parked in his driveway, Chico opened fire with the .38 revolver. Although he fired multiple times, curiously, only one ricocheting bullet struck Watson – hitting him in his upper rear left leg. Startled, frightened, bleeding, and in pain, Watson attempted to escape his attacker by running into the yard. But there was no way that this wounded, medically compromised 70-year-old man was going to outrun his 23-year-old assailant. Consequently, Watson only made it a short distance into the yard before Chico – after reloading his revolver at the edge of the driveway[202] – caught up to him. Chico then forcefully struck Watson in the face with the butt of the gun and knocked him to the ground.[203] Chico then calmly stood over Watson, assumed a shooting stance, and fired twice into Watson's upper torso.

Although Watson was still alive, Chico needed to conceal his body. Thus, Chico dragged him feet-first into a thicket of bushes that surrounded a shed located just off the driveway. Once there, Chico – still angry at the man whose ultimatum had threatened to send him back to prison – pummeled Watson's face repeatedly with the butt of the gun causing multiple lacerations and skull fractures.[204] But again,

---

[202] Investigators later found six .38 shell casings in close proximity to one another on the driveway.

[203] The ball cap that Watson habitually wore when he left his home was later found in the upper branches of a nearby tree. Chico's blow to Watson's face had dislodged the cap and flung it skyward. Crime lab analysts later confirmed that the blood found on the underside of the brim of this cap was Watson's.

[204] Dr. Mark Koponen, the medical examiner who performed the autopsy of Watson's body, would later testify that these blows had dislodged several of Watson's teeth and had driven the jagged edges of his fractured skull into the underlying brain tissue causing a subdural hematoma. He

despite his injuries, Watson was still alive. Within minutes, however, Watson's internal bleeding would cause his heart to stop beating. After 70 years of life, John Henry Watson was dead. And it was no coincidence that his death occurred on "ultimatum day."[205]

Meanwhile, Johnson, as he had been instructed to do, returned at around 9:00am and picked up Chico near a duplex parking lot across the street from Watson's house. One of the duplex residents, who had heard gunshots earlier that morning, looked out to see a blue Cadillac and two young black men. Her general descriptions of the two men fit those of Terrell and Johnson although she was never able to make a positive identification of either. Chico and his cousin then returned to the motel, checked out, bought clothes at a local department store, and returned to Barbara Terrell's house. As Chico entered the house on his way to take a shower, he spoke briefly with his mother – again claiming that he didn't have any money to repay Watson. Johnson, as he was instructed to do by Chico, washed the blue Cadillac. And later that morning, Chico and his uncle drove to the Atlanta Zoo where Chico allegedly disposed of the murder weapon.

When Watson failed to show up for his dialysis appointment, the dialysis center notified Barbara who went to check on him at around 11:00am. When she was unable to get Watson to come to the door, she forced her way in – setting off the burglar alarm. When police responded to the burglar alarm, she and the responding deputy sheriff began to search for Watson in the area surrounding his house. Maybe, Barbara hoped, Watson had become disoriented after exiting his house and had simply wandered off. After a frustratingly long search, however, they found Watson's lifeless body just before Noon.

---

further testified that the force exerted to cause these injuries was of the type typically seen in "devastating car accidents."

[205] Trial lawyers are fond of themes. In this case, my theme was "Ultimatum Day."

142

The gruesome crime scene left no doubt as to the manner of death –
this was a homicide.

Local law enforcement quickly assembled a crack team of investigators. Legendary GBI Crime Scene Tech Agent Sam House worked
the crime scene for 24 straight hours.[206] And in the days that followed,
Newton County Sheriff's Investigator Dell Reed and GBI Agent Troy
Pierce pieced together a trail of evidence that led directly to Chico
Terrell. That evidence included the fact that Terrell had recently stolen
and forged Watson's checks, had spent the night before the murder
in a motel curiously close to Watson's home, and was the only person
known to have a motive to want Watson dead. Terrell and Johnson
were soon arrested and charged with Watson's murder.[207] And after
reviewing the evidence, especially the heinous nature of Terrell's attack
on a defenseless old man, I announced that the State would seek the
death penalty.[208]

Little did I know then that I had just committed myself to a
process that would play out over the next 23 years!

In March of 1994, after almost 2 years of pretrial motion hearings,[209] and after having made a deal with Jermaine Johnson to tes-

---

[206] Special Agent Sam House was known to his fellow agents as "Mr. GBI."

[207] John Strauss, a former Alcovy Circuit District Attorney, was appointed to represent Chico.
Strauss was an experienced death penalty lawyer having both prosecuted and defended such cases.

[208] I was very sensitive to the history of racial disparities in the seeking of and imposition of death
sentences in Georgia (and elsewhere). In the Terrell case, it would be obvious to all, however, that
race was not a factor in my decision to seek the death penalty as both the victim and the suspects
were black. On the other hand, my decision to seek the death penalty may have been historic. I
have reason to believe that I was the first District Attorney in the history of the Alcovy Circuit to
seek the death penalty in a case involving a black victim.

[209] It is not unusual for defendants in death penalty cases to file over 100 motions that must be
resolved before the trial. Most are boilerplate in nature, i.e., generic and having little to do with
the facts in the case. For example, a defendant might file a "Motion to Prohibit Courtroom

143

tify against his cousin,[210] the Terrell case was ready for trial. On the eve of the trial, however, the *Covington News* printed a front-page article that detailed Terrell's past criminal history – something that trial jurors could not be told until *after* the guilt/innocence phase.[211] Consequently, Terrell's attorney filed a motion for a change of venue. The jury pool, he claimed, had been poisoned. Judge Sorrells reserved judgment, but when it was determined that a large percentage of the jurors summoned for jury duty had read this article, Judge Sorrells had no choice but to grant Terrell's motion.

Judge Sorrells was not pleased. He even summoned the Editor of the *Covington News*, Alice Queen, to his courtroom whereupon a debate pitting "the right to a fair trial" versus "the freedom of the press" ensued. This was, of course, a purely academic exercise. The trial would have to be held elsewhere. So, after searching for a jurisdiction with similar demographics to Newton County, Judge Sorrell's selected Houston County as the site for Terrell's trial. And just three months later, the trial would commence at the Houston County Courthouse in Perry, Georgia, just south of Macon, Georgia.[212]

Trying a case away from my office in Newton County turned out to be quite a logistical challenge. We not only had to transport all

---

Bailiffs from Wearing Their Police Uniforms," or a "Motion to Prohibit the State from Saying the Word 'Murder'."

[210] Johnson was a petty thief who looked up to his older cousin. He was a follower, not a leader. Hence, I was convinced that he had only done what Chico told him to do. In return for a 5-year prison sentence, Johnson agreed to cooperate and testify against Chico. His account of the crime was consistent with what we already knew and provided some essential details that we didn't know.

[211] Once a defendant in a death penalty case is found guilty, the State may present evidence in aggravation during the sentencing phase – including evidence of the defendant's criminal history. But the State may not generally do so before the defendant has been found guilty.

[212] Frankly, all I knew about Perry, Georgia, at that time was that it was the home of former U.S. Senator Sam Nunn.

of our files and evidence to an unfamiliar courthouse, but we also had to arrange transportation for the two dozen witnesses whose testimony would be needed during the trial. My investigators, Herman Bradford and Otis Harper, provided invaluable assistance. Bradford would shuttle a day's worth of witnesses from Covington to Perry each morning and return them to Covington that night. Harper would look after these witnesses' needs during the day and shepherd them to the courtroom when it was their turn to testify. Thanks to their efforts, the trial went off without a hitch.

During the trial, Investigator Reed, Agent Pierce, Harper, and I stayed at a modest Hampton Inn near I-75. (Judge Sorrells and his staff and Terrell's defense attorney stayed at the more upscale New Perry Hotel.) We ate takeout lunches from Subway, ate our dinners at a Perkins restaurant, and held midnight strategy sessions at a Waffle House. And one evening, we all sat mesmerized in my hotel room watching the infamous O. J. Simpson slow-speed white Bronco chase on live TV. Surrounded by these law enforcement professionals, I felt the kind of comradery that I had not experienced since the Jimmy Norton case.[213]

As with most of my death penalty cases, it took about 3 days to select a jury. Each prospective juror had to be questioned individually in the judge's chamber to determine if they could fairly consider both of the sentencing options – death and life imprisonment. Any prospective juror who stated that his or her views about the death penalty, pro or con, would "substantially impair" his or her ability to render a fair and impartial verdict was disqualified. And any prospective juror who stated that they would not consider both sentencing options was also

---

[213] See Chapter 3 - Murder & Manslaughter, The Jimmy Norton Case.

disqualified. Once a jury of twelve plus two alternates was selected, the trial began.

A key part of the State's case against Terrell was presenting evidence to corroborate Jermaine Johnson's testimony. We knew that Johnson's credibility would be attacked given the fact that he had made a plea deal with the State to avoid the death penalty. Fortunately, we were able to corroborate Johnson's testimony in several ways. One, the motel manager where the two had stayed the night before the murder testified that she saw Johnson, but *not* Terrell, get into a blue Cadillac and leave the motel shortly before 9:00am. This was consistent with Johnson's testimony that he had returned to the motel to take a nap before leaving to pick up Terrell – *after* the murder. She also testified that she noticed broken glass in the parking lot, but curiously, the glass was located on the *opposite side* of the car from the car's broken window. This testimony enabled me to argue that the Cadillac must have been moved *earlier* that morning – when Johnson and Terrell had left together. Two, a convenience store manager testified that she saw a man fitting Johnson's description make several trips to her store that morning in a blue Cadillac. Each time, the Cadillac had approached her store from the direction of Watson's house on Highway 142. This allowed me to argue that what she had seen was Johnson driving past Watson's house several times waiting for Terrell to appear at the road to be picked up.[214]

Although these witnesses corroborated Johnson and lent credibility to his testimony regarding Terrell's whereabouts that morning, it was Agent House's testimony that actually placed Terrell *at* the crime scene. Investigators were initially baffled when Agent House's analysis

---

[214] Johnson testified that when drove back to Watson's house to pick Terrell up that morning, he didn't see Terrell on the first several passes, and that each time, he had to turn around at a convenience store.

of the crime scene determined that 5 of the 6 bullets fired from the corner of Watson's garage had *ricocheted* off the driveway.[215] Why had the shooter, in such close proximity to his target, only been able to hit Watson with just one, ricocheting bullet? Agent House provided a theory: When he inked and rolled Terrell's fingerprints at the jail, he noticed that Terrell, who was right-handed, had an injured (or congenitally deformed) right wrist that sharply limited its range of motion. Agent House would later testify and demonstrate to the jury that given this injury (deformity), the barrel of a gun held by Terrell in his right hand would tend to point *downward* - thus explaining the ricochets! This testimony seemed to catch Terrell's lawyer completely off guard – my plan all along. But more importantly, Terrell and his lawyer *never* attempted to rebut Agent House's testimony.[216]

Unfortunately, after 9 long days, the first trial ended in a mistrial when the jury could not reach a unanimous verdict in the guilt-innocence phase. They split 9-3 for guilty.

So, what went wrong? Without taking anything away from Mr. Strauss' skillful cross-examination of the State's witnesses – especially Jermaine Johnson, I think the answer lies in the selection of the jury. Until 2005, Georgia law gave defendants twice as many peremptory strikes as the State. This meant that of the 42 qualified prospective jurors, Terrell was able to strike (excuse) 20, whereas I was only able to strike 10.[217] As a result of this numerical disadvantage, I was forced to

---

[215] These ricocheting bullets left distinctive, directional striations on the surface of the driveway. Agent House located a sixth bullet embedded in the sod just beyond the edge of the driveway near Watson's truck.

[216] If Terrell had taken the stand and, contrary to Agent House's theory, shown the jury that his right wrist was as limber as a pine needle, we would still be wiping egg off our faces. Just ask Christopher Darden and Marcia Clark about O.J. and "the glove."

[217] Thanks to a 2005 amendment to Georgia's jury selection statute, the State and defendant now enjoy "equal strikes." See O.C.G.A. §15-12-165.

"accept" two jurors who had misdemeanor marijuana convictions in their pasts – not to mention extensive tattooing of their forearms and biceps. And guess what? These two jurors were two of the three jurors who held out for acquittal! I also believe that changes of venue, in general, typically benefit the accused. Why? Because jurors selected from the transfer county tend to be less "invested" in the outcome – after all, the crime didn't occur in "their" community and the victim was not one of "theirs."

Given how close we had come to securing a unanimous verdict, I quickly announced my decision to retry the case and to again seek the death penalty. Judge Sorrells again granted a change of venue, but this time he selected Walton County[218] as the site for the second trial. Mr. Strauss objected to this choice because Jermaine Johnson had grown up in Walton County. He was also concerned that some of the prospective jurors may have read about the first trial in the *Covington News* because that newspaper had some subscribers in Walton County. Voir dire later revealed, however, that Strauss' concerns were unfounded as none of the prospective jurors knew Johnson or had read or even heard about the case.

The second Terrell trial began in Walton County in January of 1995. This time, the result would be very different. After a week-long trial, Terrell was found guilty of the murder of John Henry Watson. We were then able to proceed for the first time to the second phase – the penalty phase. At this phase, I presented evidence of two statutory aggravating circumstances. The first alleged that the offense of murder was committed while Terrell was engaged in the commission of an aggravated battery, i.e., the infliction of disfiguring injuries to Watson's body prior to his death. The second alleged that the offense of murder

---

[218] Walton County is the "sister county" to Newton County in the Alcovy Circuit.

was outrageously or wantonly vile, horrible or inhuman. I was also able to present additional evidence in aggravation, namely, certified copies of Terrell's prior criminal convictions – including the Dekalb County armed robbery, and the fact that he had set a fire in his cell block at the Newton County Jail while awaiting trial. Terrell, on the other hand, was able to present mitigating evidence through the testimony of a parade of ministers and family members who pleaded with the jury to show mercy. And then, it was in the hands of the jury.

A knock on the jury room door indicated that the jury had reached a verdict. In my Circuit, it was tradition for the jury's verdict form to be handed to the prosecutor to be read in open court. It doesn't get much more dramatic than that. And I'm not ashamed to say that when I was handed the jury's verdict form, my hands were shaking. As I flipped through the multi-page verdict form, my eyes landed on the fill-in-the-blank line on the third page where the jury had written their recommendation: D-E-A-T-H. And under Georgia law, the jury's recommendation was binding on the trial judge. As a consequence, Terrell was sentenced to death. And before long, he would find himself housed on Georgia's infamous Death Row at the Jackson Diagnostic Center in Jackson, Georgia.

In Georgia, appeals are automatic in death penalty cases. It took several years, however, before the Terrell case finally made it to the Georgia Supreme Court.[219] Terrell's appellate brief alleged over 40 enumerations of error. To address all of these enumerations, my responsive brief was 99 pages long! One of Terrell's enumerations was an obscure

---

[219] The delay was due largely to a post-trial motion filed by Strauss to recuse Judge Sorrells. Strauss questioned Judge Sorrell's continued impartiality after Sorrells vociferously objected to the defense team's post-trial testing of the jury room. Strauss had directed two of his investigators to assess the jury room's sound-proofing capabilities without first obtaining Sorrells' permission. Judge Sorrells eventually agreed to step aside to allow the appeal to move forward. For a more detailed account of this sound-proofing kerfuffle, see Chapter 14 – The Halls of Justice.

claim alleging that Judge Sorrells had erred in permitting a National Guardsman assigned to a military police unit to serve on the panel from which the trial jury was selected.[220] At the time of Terrell's trial, a defendant had the right, upon request, to exclude from jury service a *full-time police officer with arrest powers*. No case, however, had ever addressed the eligibility of a National Guardsman to serve on a criminal jury.

In November of 1999, while I was trying another death penalty case, I received a fax from the Georgia Supreme Court notifying me that it had reversed Terrell's conviction and death sentence based *solely* upon the aforementioned – seemingly trivial – jury selection error.[221] This decision hit me like a ton of bricks. There was, however, a silver lining in the Georgia Supreme Court's otherwise devastating opinion. It held that the State's evidence had been sufficient to sustain *both* Terrell's conviction and the jury's recommendation of death. Thus, the State was authorized to retry the case – for the third time.

I was determined not to let this setback obscure the *truth*, or to sully the *honor* of those who had worked so hard to resolve this case, or to deprive the Watson family of their *justice*. After all, truth, honor, and justice are more than just words; they represent ideals that are worth fighting for. So, I announced that the State would once again seek the death penalty.

Terrell's third trial would again take place in Walton County. Ironically, it was set to begin in January of 2001, just a few weeks after

---

[220] This juror was not actually selected to serve on Terrell's jury. In fact, because this juror was positioned toward the end of the qualified panel of 42, Strauss didn't even have to use one of his 20 peremptory strikes before the 12-person jury was selected!

[221] This illustrates why death penalty litigation is so difficult. Appellate courts are under extreme pressure to reverse convictions for even the slightest irregularity. This was a 6-1 decision with Justice Carley writing for the majority and with Justice Hunstein writing the lone dissent. See Terrell v. State, 271 Ga. 783 (1999).

my last term as District Attorney had ended. So, this time I would try the Terrell case as an assistant district attorney. And this time, I was faced with several new, complicating factors: Two of my witnesses – including GBI Agent Troy Pierce – had died.[222] My plea deal with Jermaine Johnson had expired following the completion of his 5-year prison sentence. This meant that I could no longer use Johnson's murder charge as leverage to secure his cooperation.[223] And all of my trial-weary witnesses would be required to testify for the third time – *8 years* after the crime. Would deceased witnesses, expired plea deals, faded memories, and the passage of time weaken the State's case?

The third trial resembled the first two trials with a few notable exceptions. The biggest of these was the fact that Terrell changed his defense strategy. In the first two trials, Mr. Strauss claimed that Terrell didn't know who had killed Watson. Strauss pointed blame, however, at a host of other possible perpetrators, including people to whom Watson allegedly owed gambling debts. He even suggested that Watson's own children might have had him killed in order to collect an early inheritance! In the third trial, however, a well-dressed, articulate Chico Terrell took the witness stand for the first time and testified that he knew the identity of the killer all along – it was his cousin Jermaine![224]

---

[222] Agent Pierce had succumbed to injuries he suffered in a car accident while returning home from a law enforcement training course. His name appears on a Memorial at the Georgia Public Safety Training Center in Forsyth, Georgia, dedicated to officers who lost their lives in the line of duty.

[223] I could, however, still force him to testify and prosecute him for perjury if he changed his testimony in any material respect from that he had given in the first two trials. Surprisingly, Johnson's testimony in the third trial was, for the most part, consistent with his previous testimony.

[224] The headline in The Covington News read: "Terrell Takes the Stand in Surprise Defense Maneuver." Terrell also claimed that he had borrowed $7000 from his father to repay Watson and thus had no reason to kill him. But from June of 1992 until his trial in 2001, he never produced or otherwise accounted for the whereabouts of this $7000. Moreover, his own mother testified

In my closing argument, I asked the jury to closely examine Terrell's new theory. Did they truly believe that Terrell was the kind of self-sacrificing person who would wait 8 long years under suspicion of murder and facing the death penalty before sharing with the world that he knew *all along* that it was his cousin Jermaine who had killed Watson? Would he really suffer those 8 years in silence when he held the key to his freedom? And if Jermaine did do it, what was his motive? Jermaine didn't owe Watson $8700. Jermaine wasn't facing a revocation of his parole and a return to prison. Watson hadn't issued Jermaine an ultimatum with a Monday, June 22nd deadline. No, I argued, it was no coincidence that Watson was killed on "Ultimatum Day." And Terrell was the only person with a motive to kill him *that* day.

Fortunately, the jury saw through Terrell's 11th hour "Hail Mary" and found him guilty.

In the sentencing phase, in addition to the two statutory aggravating circumstances that I had alleged at the second trial, I presented the jury with evidence of a new one: that the murder was committed during the commission of an armed robbery. During the guilt-innocence phase, I had shown jurors a photograph of Watson's body taken at the crime scene which revealed that Watson's pants pockets had been turned out. And Agent House had testified that, upon his inspection, both of these pockets were empty. And according to several witnesses, including Barbara Terrell, Watson never left home without folding money in his pocket.[225] Thus, I argued that Terrell must have taken money from Watson's pocket after shooting and beating him.

---

that he had denied having the money to repay Watson as late as that Monday morning – after the crime had occurred.

[225] We proved that Watson likely had cash in his pocket that morning by introducing a bank surveillance photo showing Watson withdrawing cash from his bank the previous Saturday – just

In addition to these three statutory aggravating circumstances, I also provided the third jury with a new piece of non-statutory aggravating evidence: Years earlier, prior to a pretrial motion hearing in the case, Terrell had motioned from his holding cell for Investigator Reed to come over to talk. When Reed got within earshot, Terrell told him that if he ever got out of jail, he would rape Reed's daughter.[226] *That was the real Chico Terrell.*

After weighing the aggravating and mitigating evidence, the third jury, like the second jury, returned a recommendation of death. In my mind, this was very significant. It meant that of the last 24 jurors hearing the evidence in this case, all 24 not only believed that Terrell was guilty beyond a reasonable doubt, they believed that the only just punishment for his crime was death.

And this time, I successfully fended off all of Terrell's enumerations of error on his direct appeal. The Georgia Supreme Court affirmed the conviction and death sentence in a 7-0 decision authored by Chief Justice Norman Fletcher.[227] Thereafter, the Terrell case would move slowly through the state habeas corpus process and the federal appellate courts. Terrell's death sentence was once even set aside on habeas before being reinstated.[228] Finally, on December 9, 2015, twenty-three

---

two days before the murder. That photo also showed Watson wearing his favorite ball cap - the one found in the tree near where Terrell had first pistol-whipped Watson.

[226] I chose not to use this testimony in the second trial because Reed's daughter, who had attended school with Terrell, was still living at home and might have learned about this threat by reading the newspaper. By the time of the third trial, however, she was married and living in another state.

[227] This was a significant accomplishment because Chief Justice Fletcher was an outspoken opponent of the death penalty. See Terrell v. State, 276 Ga. 34 (2002).

[228] A state court judge ruled that Terrell's attorney had rendered ineffective assistance by not hiring an expert to challenge the state medical examiner's opinion that Watson was still alive when he received the blows to his face after being drug into the bushes. The Georgia Supreme Court, however, reversed this ruling and reinstated the sentence of death in another 7-0 decision. See Hall v. Terrell, 285 Ga. 448 (2009).

years and 163 days after the crime, Terrell was put to death by lethal injection at the Jackson Diagnostic Center in Jackson, Georgia.[229]

May John Henry Watson rest in peace.[230]

---

[229] Two days before Terrell's execution, at the invitation of District Attorney Layla Zon, I testified before the Georgia Board of Pardons & Paroles at Terrell's clemency hearing. I presented the Board with a PowerPoint summary of the case – the same one that I used for years in my class-room at UGA Law when lecturing on the death penalty.

[230] I chose not to attend the execution itself. Why not? Because at that point, I had performed all of the duties assigned to me by Georgia law. Three of the four goals of sentencing and corrections had already been achieved: deterrence, punishment, and incapacitation. The only remaining goal was retribution. And that was never about me. Retribution was for John Henry Watson and his family.

CHAPTER 11

Crimes of Unspeakable Evil

As I frequently told my law students, I was constantly *disappointed* by the things that I saw people do to their fellow human beings, but I was rarely *surprised* by them. Unfortunately, man's inhumanity toward his fellow man is not an aberration; it's been a recurring theme throughout human history. And I saw plenty during my time as a prosecutor.

We need to face the facts: Evil does exist in this world. And some people are evil. I saw this firsthand. And any person who prosecutes for any considerable length of time will see it too. And when evil is encountered, it must be met head-on. Or as the 18th-century Irish statesman Edmund Burke once said, "The only thing necessary for the triumph of evil is for good men to do nothing." So, what exactly is a prosecutor's role in confronting evil?

A prosecutor's primary duty in the criminal justice system is to fairly enforce the criminal laws that are designed to safeguard law-abiding citizens and their property – in other words, to deter and punish criminally bad behavior.[231] Surprisingly, however, this view has come under attack in recent years. More and more candidates for the office of

---

[231] The proper focus of the criminal justice system is, in many respects, no different from that of raising children. When you reward good behavior, you tend to get more of it. And when you punish bad behavior, you tend to get less of it.

District Attorney tout their "social justice" bona fides instead of their commitment to the rule of law. I fear that the result of this burgeoning social justice movement will be more lawless behavior and fewer safe communities.

Mandatory sentencing laws are one of the primary targets of this emerging social justice movement. These laws mandate that persons convicted of certain serious crimes are sentenced to lengthy prison terms – sometimes without the possibility of parole.[232] Such laws typically address society's most disturbing and destructive crimes like murder, rape, armed robbery, and drug trafficking. Those who argue against such sentencing schemes tend to ignore one simple truth: They work. Crime rates have dropped significantly since the 1990s when these sentencing schemes were first introduced. Why? Because criminals who commit these kinds of crimes are almost always poor candidates for rehabilitation. Thus, by keeping them locked up for longer periods of time, we achieve a reduced rate of recidivism – and likely save many lives in the process.

Don't get me wrong, I applaud the increasing use of so-called "accountability courts" whose goal is to rehabilitate young, non-violent, first-time offenders, e.g., drug courts, mental health courts, veteran's courts, etc. And I support programs for probationers, inmates, and parolees that teach life skills and provide job training. But I reject the argument that every criminal can be rehabilitated. Some simply can't.

---

[232] Mandatory life without parole in Georgia is typically reserved for habitually violent criminals. For example, Georgia's Two Strikes Law provides that upon a person's second conviction for a serious violent felony like murder, rape, kidnapping, or armed robbery, he must be sentenced to life without the possibility of parole. See O.C.G.A. §17-10-7.

Or as I once read, society shouldn't expect to rehabilitate someone who was never "habilitated" in the first place.[233]

In a time when our criminal justice system is under attack for being too punitive and incarcerating too many people, I think that we should not lose sight of the fact that the overarching goal of the criminal justice system is public safety – not social engineering. And that some offenders – even some young first-time offenders – don't deserve a second chance. For them, rehabilitation is not a realistic goal. For these offenders – regardless of their troubled childhoods, drug addiction, or "woe is me" sob stories – a second chance poses an unacceptable risk of harm to the law-abiding public.

The defendants in the cases described below committed crimes of unspeakable evil and deserved no second chances.[234]

The Smith, Momom, & Ramey Case[235]

Angie, an 18-year-old girl, and her 14-year-old brother Jacob (not their real names) were traveling from their home in North Carolina to visit Angie's boyfriend in Alabama when their car broke down on I-20 in Newton County. They walked to a nearby gasoline station where three men – Tyrone Smith, Tarell Momom, and Willie Claude Ramey[236] – overheard them talking about their predicament. One of these men offered to give them a ride back to their car and to take a look under

---

[233] This quote is attributable to forensic psychologist Dr. Stanton Samenow. See https://www.psychologytoday.com/us/blog/inside-the-criminal-mind/201512/in-2016-habilitation-not-rehabilitation

[234] The following cases described in other chapters could just as easily have been included in this chapter: The David Huggins Case and The William Walsh Case in Chapter 2; The Jimmy Norton Case in Chapter 3; The Brian "Chico" Terrell Case in Chapter 10.

[235] Smith v. State, A01A1341, August 31, 2001 (not officially reported); Ramey v. State, 235 Ga. App. 690 (1998).

[236] Ramey was in his 30's; Smith and Momom were teenagers.

the hood. Angie and Jacob didn't have enough money to afford a tow truck or car repairs, so they naively accepted the man's offer.

As they left the gasoline station, Smith drove, Momom was in the front passenger seat, and Ramey, Angie, and Jacob rode in the backseat – with Angie seated in the middle. When they reached Angie's abandoned car, Ramey got out and tinkered under the hood for a few minutes before announcing that he couldn't fix it. Almost immediately thereafter, Momom pulled a gun and pointed it at Angie and Jacob. "Suckers!," he said. And for the next few hours, Angie and Jacob were taken on a harrowing ride on unfamiliar rural backroads. Along the way, Smith and Momom threatened to kill them and taunted them with racial epithets – calling them, among other things, "crackers." And Ramey repeatedly touched Angie between her legs and only stopped when she told him that she was on her menstrual period.

When the sun went down, Smith finally stopped the car on a deserted dirt road. And that's when the real nightmare for Angie and Jacob began. Momon got out first and handed the gun to Ramey. One of the men then ordered Jacob and Angie to get out of the car and to take off their clothes. Ramey then held the gun on Jacob as Smith and Momom took turns orally and anally sodomizing Angie. Powerless to intervene, Jacob was forced to watch as his sister was being sexually assaulted just a few feet away. When Smith and Momom were finally satiated, they repeatedly threatening to shoot Angie and Jacob before suddenly getting back into the car and driving away.

Angie and Jacob had been left naked and barefooted in the pitch-dark night. Feeling their way through the darkness, they eventually saw a faint light coming from a distant farmhouse. They followed this light for almost a mile. And when they finally reached the farmhouse, they pounded on the door and cried for help. The horror-struck residents took them in, wrapped them in blankets, and called police. Angie and

Jacob, despite having endured unimaginable physical and mental torture, were very lucky to be alive.

All three men were later identified from the security video at the gasoline station where they had initially met up with Angie and Jacob. They were all arrested, charged, prosecuted, and convicted.[237] And all three men received lengthy prison sentences. In a classic Judge "Maximum Marvin" Sorrells sentencing hearing in Smith's case, the following exchange occurred:

> Sorrells: On Count 1, I sentence you to 20 years confinement. On Count 2, I sentence you to 20 years confinement, *consecutive* to Count 1 ... that's 40 years. On Count 3, I sentence you to 20 years confinement, *consecutive* to Count 2 ... that's 60 years. [Before Judge Sorrells was done, he had sentenced Smith to 115 years in prison.]
>
> Mr. Smith, do you have any questions about your sentence?
>
> Smith: 115 years? You fat son of a bitch!
>
> Sorrells: Well, I have put on a little weight lately. [Patting his stomach]
>
> [To deputy] Take him back [to the jail].

As Smith was being led from the courtroom, Jacob, who was present during the exchange above, leaped to his feet and yelled, "Who's the 'cracker' now, you motherf-----!" After Smith had been removed from the courtroom, Judge Sorrells told the young man that he ordinarily

---

[237] Momom pled guilty. Smith and Ramey pled not guilty and were tried separately.

held people in contempt of court for such outbursts, but this time, given what he and his sister had endured, he would let it slide.

* * *

In 2019, while sitting in my office at the Law School, I received a phone call out of the blue from Jacob. The then 38-year-old married father of three wanted to know if the three men who had terrorized him and his sister were still in prison. While we were on the phone, I looked up their status on the Department of Corrections website and was able to advise Jacob that all three men were still in prison. I told Jacob that Ramey, who had been sentenced to life, would likely spend the remainder of his days in prison. Smith still had 92 years remaining on his 115-year sentence. And, most surprising of all, Momom, the youngest of the three who had pled guilty and received the shortest sentence, had killed a fellow inmate in prison and been sentenced to life without parole!

So, yes, evil does exist. And if the death penalty is not imposed, there's only one safe place for evil-doers like Smith, Momom, and Ramey: prison.[238]

The William Posey Case

Wendy (not the child's real name) feared that *it* was about to happen again.

This 9-year-old child's stepfather would frequently take her to his bedroom after lunch and touch her inappropriately. But this time, it would be different. She had a plan. As her mother cleared the dishes from the table, Wendy suddenly darted for the back door.

---

[238] Rape cases were once eligible for the death penalty. But in Coker v. Georgia (1977), the U.S. Supreme Court held that the death penalty may only be imposed in murder cases.

Once outside, she hopped on her bicycle and peddled as fast as she could toward downtown Monroe. Would he follow her? No, but her mother did – pursuing Wendy in the family car for several blocks. Fortunately, Wendy was able to flag down a lady in a downtown parking lot before her mother could catch up to her. This kind stranger listened to Wendy's frantic pleas for help, loaded Wendy's bicycle into her car, and drove Wendy to the Monroe Police Department.

The investigation that followed revealed a shocking tale of child abuse.

Wendy's stepfather, Willard Posey, had met Wendy's mother, Joyce, several years previously at a Waffle House in Alabama where Joyce worked as a waitress. Joyce was 20 years his junior and was in a troubled, abusive marriage. When Posey learned that Joyce had two daughters, aged 9 and 6, and had separated from her husband, he offered to let her and her daughters stay in his home.[239] Out of sheer desperation, simple naivety, or perhaps both, Joyce accepted his offer. And when Joyce's divorce became final, Posey asked her to marry him and she agreed to do so. As she would later testify, she felt obligated to marry him because he had "rescued" her from a bad marriage. And before long, Joyce and Posey would have a child of their own – a baby boy.

Tragically – and what any trained child abuse professional could have easily predicted – Posey began to molest Joyce's older daughter. And after a few years, he turned his lascivious attentions toward Wendy as well. During this time, the Posey's moved several times from Alabama to Florida, from Florida back to Alabama, and from Alabama to Georgia – always just a step ahead of Child Services. And in 1998,

---

[239] I can't tell you how many times I saw this predatory practice in my child abuse cases: Man targets single woman with young female children and …

the Posey's settled in the City of Monroe in Walton County. Posey got a job as a handyman for a string of low-rent tenement houses. Joyce was a stay-at-home mom. And to avoid the risk that his illicit activities might be detected, Posey insisted that the children be home-schooled.

What Posey hadn't counted on, however, was Wendy's courageous and ultimately successful escape attempt.

When the two sisters were interviewed at the police station, they each provided detailed accounts of their sexual abuse at the hands of their stepfather.[240] The particulars are too graphic to describe here, but suffice it to say that most of the alleged sex acts involved objects that investigators later seized during the execution of a search warrant at Posey's house. And that wasn't all that investigators found. They found what would later become my all-time favorite trial exhibit: a magazine in Posey's bedroom closet titled *Family Love* that was entirely devoted to and glorified incest. Yes, you read that correctly.

As disturbing as these allegations against Posey were, there was another equally disturbing aspect of this case: Wendy told investigators that her mother, Joyce, was not only aware of Posey's abuse, she had *participated* in it. Specifically, Wendy told investigators that when she resisted her stepfather's advances, her mother would hold her down or sit on her. And in Joyce's subsequent statement to police, she didn't deny Wendy's allegation. She did, however, attempt to minimize her participation and blameworthiness by suggesting that she was only attempting to "comfort" her daughter.[241]

---

[240] My Circuit did not have a Child Advocacy Center with trained child forensic interviewers in the 1990s. Our child interviews were typically conducted either by a Department of Family & Child Services (DFCS) caseworker or a police investigator. A few of my favorite child interviewers were Sherri Asbil, Jackie Ellis, and Kathy Herrin (Newton DFCS); Gwen Hightower (NCSO); Melinda Quinn and Evelyn Bates (Walton DFCS).

[241] Joyce was herself a victim of sexual abuse as a child. She had also been physically abused by her first husband and clearly dominated by Posey. Nonetheless, she had a duty as a mother to protect

When the Posey girls and their 3-year-old brother were examined by a pediatrician that afternoon, the pediatrician[242] observed visible physical injuries consistent with sexual abuse on *all three* of the Posey children. This came as somewhat of a shock to the investigators. As any child abuse professional will tell you, discovering corroborating medical evidence in a child sexual abuse case is extremely rare. Why? Because child victims often wait for months, if not years, before telling anyone about their abuse. As a result of these so-called "delayed disclosures," most soft tissue injuries will have healed by the time an outcry is made. Moreover, because most child molesters "groom" their victims gradually, their sex acts directed at children are rarely forceful and rarely leave physical marks or scars.

After a brief investigation, both Posey and Joyce were arrested and charged with the offense of child molestation. When police interrogated Posey and confronted him with Wendy's allegations, he was indignant. Having attended a few years of college, Posey claimed to be well-educated. He also claimed to be a lay minister. When asked why Wendy would make up such a horrific story about him, he said that she was lying because he had punished her for not doing her chores. And as for Joyce, he told investigators that they couldn't trust anything she said because she was "slow" and incapable of understanding even simple things. The entire situation, according to Posey, was all just a big misunderstanding.

After reviewing the investigative file, including the corroborating medical report, I concluded that this case was a slam dunk winner.

---

her children and she failed miserably.

[242] Dr. Caratao had received specialized training in detecting the signs of child sexual abuse as an intern at a New York City hospital. After diagnosing the children in the Posey case, she moved her practice to California but fully cooperated when I needed her to return for the trial of the case. She was an amazing witness.

The evidence against Posey was overwhelming. Consequently, I had no reason to offer him a plea bargain to induce him to plead guilty – and I didn't. My goals were simple: (1) to put Posey away for life, and (2) to wrest permanent custody of these children away from *both* Posey and their mother, Joyce. To accomplish this, I offered Joyce a plea deal: testify against your husband, surrender your parental rights, and receive a reduced sentence of 5 years in prison.

When Posey became aware of my plea offer to Joyce, he was irate. He thereafter engaged in a prolific letter-writing campaign to convince her that if they stuck together, they could beat the charges and get their kids back. Since he and Joyce were both housed at the Walton County Jail, his correspondence to her didn't have to travel far. But unbeknownst to Posey, the jail intercepted these letters, and I was able to read every one of them.[243] When Posey finally realized what was going on, he started including at least one paragraph in his letters to Joyce addressed to me. For example: "Mr. Cook, I'm going to report you to the State Bar, sue you for malicious prosecution, and collect one million dollars in damages" and the like. (He never followed through on his threats.) Despite his efforts, Joyce eventually accepted my terms, waived her spousal testimonial privilege, and agreed to testify against her husband.

Because Wendy was very frightened at the prospect of having to testify in Posey's presence,[244] I filed a motion to present her testimony

---

[243] Pursuant to a well-recognized exception to the 4th Amendment's search warrant requirement, such communications between inmates may be seized without a search warrant in order to maintain safe and secure jails, e.g., to ensure that inmates aren't plotting an escape, assault, riot, etc. (Communications between inmates and their lawyers, of course, are exempt from this exception.)

[244] Prior to Posey's arrest, he and Wendy had a chance encounter at their home when a police officer and a DFCS caseworker brought Wendy there to retrieve her clothes. When Posey saw her, he sternly warned her, "You be a good girl, you don't have to tell them [the police] nothing!"

via closed-circuit TV.[245] Posey was again apoplectic. He was insistent that he be allowed to "confront his accuser" face-to-face. I think he knew that intimidating Wendy on the witness stand in open court was his best and perhaps only chance of acquittal. Fortunately, after hearing testimony from Wendy's child therapist, the court granted my motion. Thus, we were able to broadcast Wendy's closed-circuit testimony at trial from the relative calm of the judge's chambers. And her testimony was riveting.

Posey was thereafter convicted and sentenced to fifty (50) years in prison.

* * *

When someone is sentenced to prison in Georgia, the Pardons & Paroles Board launches an immediate investigation into the prisoner's background and character. As a part of this investigation, the prosecutor is typically invited to share his or her opinion about the prisoner. Once this report is completed, it is filed away until the inmate becomes eligible to apply for early release. It can then be reviewed by the Board. In my letter to the Parole Board, I wrote:

> This defendant is the most vile, horrible, wicked, sinister, conniving, manipulating, disgusting, and evil child molester I have ever had the pleasure of putting behind bars. The State strongly encourages the Board to require this inmate to serve every day of his sentence or until he dies in prison, whichever comes first, hopefully the latter.

---

[245] In Maryland v. Craig (1990), the United States Supreme Court carved out an exception to a defendant's right to confront his accuser in open court when the "necessities of the case" require it – such as when a child is so fearful of testifying in the defendant's presence that his or her ability to effectively communicate would be significantly compromised.

* * *

Following the trial, the Poseys' parental rights were terminated in the Juvenile Court and all three children were adopted by a couple from Dekalb. Fortuitously, a few years later, I saw them walking with their new parents at the Dekalb Mall. That is when I knew that my goals in the Posey case had been fully accomplished – that and the fact that William Posey later died in prison.[246]

---

[246] Curiously, Posey never pursued a direct appeal of his conviction.

CHAPTER 12

The CSI Effect

Since the 1990s, TV shows like *CSI* and *Forensic Files* have highlighted the ability of law enforcement to solve crimes using forensic evidence, e.g., DNA, fingerprints, fiber analysis, ballistics, etc. Although the public's fascination with crime-fighting and investigative techniques is generally a good thing, their obsession with these TV shows has led to what prosecutors today call the "*CSI* Effect."

The *CSI* Effect is perhaps best explained as the tendency of trial jurors to expect, if not insist upon, the presentation of forensic evidence in *every* case. In my experience, for example, it was not uncommon for prospective jurors to say – especially during voir dire in death penalty cases – that they might not be able to vote to convict a defendant in the absence of DNA or other definitive forensic proof.

The simple truth, however, is that most crimes are not solved by DNA or any other forensic evidence. Most crimes are solved with good, old-fashioned witness testimony that places the offender at the scene of the crime with the motive and means to commit it. Nonetheless, prosecutors today act at their own peril if they ignore the desire and expectation of modern jurors for scientific proof of a defendant's guilt. And juries will hold police and prosecutors accountable if they don't at least try to gather forensic evidence or explain why there was none to be found.

The following cases illustrate some of the many ways that cases can be solved – some with and some without forensic evidence – and why police and prosecutors cannot afford to rely on, and jurors should not insist upon, any one investigative technique or category of evidence.

The Terry Ross "Latent Fingerprint" Case[247]

Fingerprint analysis – which originated in the 1850's – was perhaps the first of the forensic techniques used to solve crimes. Yet in my almost 14 years as a prosecutor, I can only recall two cases that were solved by fingerprint evidence. The following case is one of them.

Kevin Little, who would later become the Chairman of the Walton County Board of Commissioners, lived in a remote rural part of Walton County. One day, he came home to discover that the storage building behind his house had been broken into and that some of his race car equipment had been stolen. Unfortunately, daytime home burglaries are notoriously difficult to solve because there is rarely an eyewitness present to describe the burglar or his means of transportation. And even if a suspect is later found in possession of the stolen goods, he can always claim that he acquired them unwittingly from a third party.[248]

In this case, however, a meticulous crime scene technician took the time to lift latent fingerprints off one of the cars that Little had left in his driveway that day. Was it possible that the burglar had touched

---

[247] Ross v. State, 199 Ga. App. 767 (1991).

[248] I can't count the number of times that a burglary or theft suspect raised the "some dude sold it to me" defense to explain their recent possession of stolen property. Of course, they could never seem to remember the name of the "dude" or give more than a vague physical description of him.

this car and left his fingerprints? It was, to say the least, a longshot.[249] Nonetheless, the tech lifted several latent prints and ran them through AFIS.[250] And surprisingly, he got a "hit." One of the latent prints belonged to a man named Terry Ross, a known criminal with a history of committing burglaries. Moreover, Ross had a prior conviction for burglarizing a garage used to work on race cars!

When police picked Ross up in another jurisdiction, they didn't tell him that they had found his fingerprints at the crime scene. Instead, they asked him just one question: "Have you ever been out to Kevin Little's house in Walton County?" Ross emphatically answered that not only had he not been to Little's house, he had not even been in Walton County in "a long, long time." That statement would prove to be Ross' undoing.

At Ross' trial, GBI Crime Lab fingerprint expert Lou Cuendet testified that Ross' fingerprint on the hood of Little's car could only have survived the elements, i.e., the hot sun, for at most 1-2 days. Thus, on the day of the burglary, Ross' fingerprint was fresh.[251] In other words, it could not have survived on the hood of Little's car for a "long, long time" before the burglary. When combined with the other incriminating evidence – including testimony pointing out the similarities between this burglary and the facts surrounding Ross' prior burglary,[252] the fingerprint evidence was enough to secure a conviction.

---

[249] Contrary to popular belief, our fingerprints are not transferred to every surface that we touch. And even if the oils or perspiration on a perpetrator's fingers leave a latent print on a receptive surface, there may be insufficient ridge detail to make a positive comparison to a suspect's known fingerprints. In fact, finger to surface contact often just leaves a smudge with no ridge detail at all.

[250] AFIS stands for the Automated Fingerprint Identification System.

[251] This reminds me of what Gil Grissom of CSI fame often said, "I tend not to believe people; they lie. But the evidence? It never lies."

[252] A defendant's prior similar or "pattern crime" may be admissible at a defendant's subsequent trial for a similar offense if "the former tends to prove the latter," e.g., when the modus operandi

"Old school" fingerprint evidence had solved the case.

The Meko Campbell "McDonald's Armed Robbery" Case[253]

I had my first "date" with my future wife at the McDonald's on Highway 278 in Covington, Georgia. Debra and I were freshmen at nearby Oxford College and had a chance encounter at the Student Center during the first two weeks of class. Because we had friends in common, she invited me to lunch. (I think I had a fish sandwich.) We've been together ever since – over 40 years now.

Fast forward to 1994. At this same McDonald's near closing time on Super Bowl Sunday, an armed man with a ski mask approached a McDonald's employee in the parking lot as she was taking out the trash. The gunman led this frightened employee back inside the restaurant at gunpoint and threatened to harm her if the assistant manager didn't open the safe. The assistant manager complied, and the gunman got away with the next day's start-up cash.[254] The gunman then fled on foot to a waiting vehicle and its getaway driver. When police arrived, one of the McDonald's employees not only gave them a description of the robber, she gave them his name! How is that possible, you ask? Read on.

The robber was a young man named Meko Campbell who had attended public schools in nearby Jasper County. Unfortunately for him, so did this McDonald's employee. When Campbell entered the restaurant that night, this employee not only recognized his voice, she also recognized his unusually large eyes peering back at her through his

---

in the two crimes are nearly identical. Here, the somewhat rare targeting of race car equipment.

[253] Campbell v. State, A95A2562, January 11, 1996 (not officially reported).

[254] The gunman also took money from the Ronald McDonald House charity jar. Classy, very classy.

ski mask. Campbell apparently also recognized the employee, for when their eyes met, he exclaimed, "Oh, shit!"

Criminal justice professionals know, however, that eyewitness identifications are notoriously unreliable. In fact, reliance on eyewitness identifications is one of the leading causes of wrongful convictions. As a result, police and prosecutors in the modern era are very reluctant to rely *solely* on such identifications. But in this case, the eyewitness making the identification actually knew the alleged perpetrator *before* the crime. And she recognized *both* his voice and his eyes. The distinction is important – like the difference between *me* identifying my neighbor and *you* doing so.

Nonetheless, to confirm that the McDonald's employee was not mistaken, investigators asked her to look at a photographic lineup of six young men fitting Campbell's general description. But unlike a standard photo lineup, the six photographs in this photo array only revealed the men's eyes – as if the six men were peering through a rectangular mail slot. When confronted with this photo lineup, the employee immediately identified the photograph of Campbell's eyes.

Investigators were also able to identify the getaway driver. While investigating a noise violation just prior to the robbery and only a few blocks from the McDonald's, a Covington Police officer stopped a car being driven by a man named Donrico Reid.[255] Reid was alone at the time. Additional investigative efforts, however, placed Reid and Campbell together that night – earlier in the City of Monticello[256] and later, after the robbery, in Covington. These corroborating facts plus

---

[255] Perhaps I should have included Reid in Chapter 7 - Stupid Crimes & Crazy Criminals. You would think that a getaway driver would turn down his car stereo so as not to attract the attention of police, right?

[256] Monticello is the county seat of Jasper County and the hometown of Country music artist Trisha Yearwood. And its courthouse was the backdrop for My Cousin Vinny.

the McDonald's employee's very convincing identification testimony led a Newton County jury to find Campbell guilty.[257]

Eyewitness testimony – here, identifying the suspect's eyes – had solved the case.[258]

The John Tinker "Professional Thief" Case[259]

Someone was breaking into high-end sporting goods stores in metro Atlanta and stealing ski equipment, tennis rackets, and other pricey items. The thief was obviously a pro. He would gain entry into these stores by entering a less secure adjacent business in a strip mall and then cutting a hole in the wall separating the two businesses.

This professional burglar had wreaked so much havoc in northeast Atlanta that a multi-jurisdictional task force was formed just to catch *him*. Eventually, the task force developed a suspect – a young man named John Tinker. Tinker and his girlfriend – who was reportedly a high-priced escort and stripper – were living at that time in an extravagant home in Walton County. According to the neighbors, Tinker and his girlfriend seemed to be living well beyond their means

---

[257] Not long ago, a student of mine alerted me to a subsequent prosecution of Campbell in 2013 – not long after his release from prison. See U.S. v. Campbell, 912 F.3d 1340 (2019). In that case, Campbell was the subject of a traffic stop. And guess what police found in his car? A 9mm semi-automatic pistol, 9mm ammunition, and a black stocking cap! I wonder what he intended to do with those? See Chapter 11 for my general thoughts about rehabilitation.

[258] Jurors rejected Campbell's alibi defense supported by his relatives who swore under oath that Campbell was in Monticello that night at a wake for a recently deceased uncle. Relatives, however, make terrible alibi witnesses because jurors are naturally suspicious that relatives might lie to protect their loved ones. Which is exactly what happened here.

[259] Tinker v. State, 218 Ga. App. 792 (1995).

and didn't seem to fit into their upscale neighborhood.[260] Thus, they reported their suspicions to the police.

With this information in hand, task force agents placed Tinker under surveillance. With a team of twenty ground-based units and an airplane to track his vehicle from the air, the agents were able to observe Tinker as he attempted to break into several businesses. And although this was only enough to charge him with criminal attempt, it was more than enough to secure a search warrant for his home. What they found inside was a treasure trove of stolen goods taken in dozens of metro Atlanta burglaries. But what turned out to be their most important discovery was a pair of Tinker's tennis shoes and one of his power tools.

GBI microanalyst Larry Peterson was able to match the shoe size and tread pattern of Tinker's shoes with several unknown shoe prints left at multiple burglary locations in the Atlanta area. And GBI criminalist Kelly Fite was able to match the broken tip of a reciprocating saw blade found at one of these locations with a broken blade shaft that was still attached to a reciprocating saw found at Tinker's home. The testimony of these two forensic experts was spellbinding. The semi-transparent overlays of Tinker's shoe prints matched the unknown shoe prints perfectly. And the magnified side-by-side comparison of the jagged edges of the broken saw blade fit like pieces of a jigsaw puzzle. The jury ate it up.

Peterson and Fite's expert opinions enabled police to link Tinker to multiple commercial burglaries in Northeast Atlanta. And shipping materials found in his home suggested that Tinker was shipping the stolen merchandise to the Northeast where it was being fenced by an associate. Together, these elements of proof allowed me to argue that

---

[260] Tinker's neighbors were also shocked and dismayed at the number of men who frequented the Tinker home and would pick up and return the "lady of the house" in a limousine at all hours of the night.

Tinker was part of a "criminal enterprise." Consequently, I was able to indict and successfully try him under Georgia's Racketeer Influenced Corrupt Organizations Act (RICO).

Citizen tips, multi-jurisdictional cooperation, advanced surveillance techniques, and forensic analysis of shoe prints and toolmarks by crime lab experts had solved the case.

* * *

Aside from being an example of stellar police work, the Tinker case was noteworthy for several other reasons. At Tinker's bond hearing, he tried to escape from the courtroom by running down and out a back stairwell. This proved difficult, however, because his hands were shackled at the waist! Deputies caught up to him before he even got to the bottom of the steps.

And in what could only be described as another Quixotic misstep, Tinker attempted to represent himself at his trial. That effort also crashed and burned when he flubbed the cross-examination of the State's first witness and inadvertently opened the door to the admissibility of his entire criminal history. Following that miscue, Tinker insisted on returning to his jail cell for the remainder of the trial and was thereafter tried in absentia.[261]

The Joseph Bishop "Kidnapping for Ransom" Case

Many Georgians remember the 1968 kidnapping of Emory University student Barbara Jane Mackle.[262] Mackle was kidnapped and buried alive in a box that was equipped with an air pump to provide her with oxygen to breathe. After her wealthy family paid a sizable ransom, the

---

[261] See fn. 153 (defining trials in absentia).

[262] Mackle wrote a book about her ordeal titled: 83 Hours Til Dawn.

kidnappers provided police with directions to locate Mackle's shallow grave. After being buried for almost three days, she was still alive. The kidnappers were later tracked down and arrested. And in 1974, there was another high-profile kidnapping for ransom case in Georgia. Reg Murphy, the editor of the *Atlanta Constitution*, was kidnapped but released after his newspaper paid the ransom. The kidnapper was arrested within hours of Murphy's release.[263]

So, what does all of this have to do with my Circuit in the 1990s? Kidnappings for ransom, like disco music, were relics from the 1970s, right? Well, as Coach Corso of *Game Day* fame might say, "Not so fast, my friend."

Joseph Bishop was strung out on drugs and down on his luck. He decided that the answer to his predicament was a bank loan. But when he applied for a loan at the National Bank of Walton County, a female bank manager turned him down. The next morning, Bishop ambushed her as she left her house, tied her hands behind her back, and placed a bag over her head. He then drove her to an abandoned house in Snellville where he hurriedly tied her to a bed frame.

Bishop then called the banker's father and instructed him to bring $30,000 to Briscoe Park in Gwinnett County or his daughter would be killed. The banker's father compliantly drove to his bank and attempted to withdraw $30,000 from his account. When bank employees expressed their concern about his making such a large withdrawal, he told him that his daughter had been kidnapped and that he had been told not to alert police. But as soon as he left the bank with the ransom money, bank employees immediately reported the situation to the Monroe Police Department (MPD).

---

[263] The Murphy kidnapping occurred just weeks after the more sensational Patty Hearst kidnapping in California.

What happened next was an extraordinarily well-coordinated law enforcement effort to catch a kidnapper. MPD investigators immediately contacted the FBI with a description of the father's car. FBI agents then called the Bureau of Alcohol, Tobacco, and Firearms (ATF) and requisitioned an airplane. FBI agents were then able to track the father's car from the sky as he made his way to Gwinnett County with the ransom money. And when Bishop approached the prearranged drop location to retrieve the money – a wastebasket in Briscoe Park, FBI agents converged and placed him under arrest.

"Where is she?" the Agents asked. Bishop, feigning ignorance, claimed that he did not know where the banker was – that she was being held by an accomplice in an undisclosed location. The FBI wasn't buying it. What happened next is not entirely clear, but when Bishop was booked into the jail, he had visible bruises on his face. When famed Atlanta criminal defense attorney Bruce Harvey later met with me to negotiate a plea agreement, he told me that Bishop claimed that the FBI agents had "roughed him up." I then asked Harvey, "Are you married?" Harvey advised me that he was and had been for over 20 years. I then asked, "Hypothetically speaking, if someone kidnapped your wife and refused to tell police where she was, would you have a problem with police using 'unconventional methods' to get an answer?" Harvey smiled and nodded his head.[264]

The evidence would later reveal that Bishop had acted alone. Fortunately, his refusal to disclose the banker's location did not result in her dying alone in the abandoned house where he had hidden her. For unbeknownst to Bishop and the FBI agents who conducted his post-arrest interrogation, the banker had managed to free herself from

---

[264] Harvey represented many high-profile defendants in his career. He is perhaps best known nationally for securing an acquittal in the case of one of the co-defendants in the Ray Lewis Super Bowl XXXIV double murder case in Atlanta.

her restraints shortly after Bishop's arrest. Once free, she walked to the Snellville Police Department and reported her own kidnapping to a no doubt bewildered intake officer. Bishop eventually pled guilty to Kidnapping for Ransom and received a life sentence.

Alert bank employees, a coordinated effort by state and federal law enforcement, advanced surveillance techniques, and the daring escape of the victim herself had solved the case.

CHAPTER 13

The Thin Blue Line[265]

Let me make one thing perfectly clear: I am pro-law enforcement. Why? Because I believe in the "rule of law." The rule of law is the only thing that stands between law-abiding citizens and anarchy. Without the rule of law, a free society could not function. And without police, adherence to the rule of law would depend upon the voluntary compliance of *all* of the people *all* of the time. Such a utopian society has never existed nor is one likely to exist in the future.

We ask our elected representatives to enact criminal laws to establish boundaries for acceptable human behavior. And to deter individuals from crossing these boundary lines, these laws provide for the imposition of punitive consequences for those who willfully choose to violate them. Unfortunately, human nature being what it is, we know that a certain proportion of our fellow citizens will ignore this threat of punishment. To them, punishment – including jail time – is just a cost of doing business. So, unless we are willing to accept vigilantism as the prescription for lawless behavior, society must have a well-trained police force to uphold the rule of law.

---

[265] The "thin blue line" is a term often used to describe the pivotal role police play in a civilized society to stand between law-abiding citizens and violent criminals.

I loved working with the men and women of law enforcement. For almost 14 years, I had a front-row seat to view their day-to-day professional activities and a behind-the-scenes look at their personal lives. I wish that the general public could see what I saw. What I learned from this unique access was that the vast majority of police officers are truly dedicated to serving and protecting the public with honor and dignity. Unfortunately, the general public's perception of the police is often unfairly shaped by what they see on the evening news – stories about the few bad apples that dishonor their badges.[266]

Courageous Cops

Many of my students entered law school with a somewhat skeptical view of police officers. Their skepticism almost invariably stemmed from a bad experience with a police officer on a routine traffic stop. "The officer was unfriendly, arrogant, and rude," they might say. Okay. I get it. No one likes to be pulled over by a cop and no one likes getting a traffic ticket. But I always made a point of explaining to my students that there is no such thing as a "routine traffic stop." Police officers cannot afford to let their guard down – not for a minute. To drive home this point, I would share with them the following true story.

Deputy Henry "Bo" Huff was on routine patrol in the Walnut Grove area of Walton County late one night when he stopped a car for speeding 88/55mph zone. It appeared to be a "routine traffic stop." As Deputy Huff approached the stopped car alongside Highway 81, the young male driver rolled down his window. As Deputy Huff began to tell the driver why he had stopped him, two loud gunshots rang out accompanied by muzzle flashes. The driver had pulled a 9mm pistol and shot the deputy twice in the chest at close range.

---

[266] Bad apples are not unique to law enforcement. I prosecuted and disbarred two attorneys during my tenure as District Attorney – one for bribery and the other for cocaine possession.

The force of the shots spun Deputy Huff around and almost knocked him to the ground. But within seconds, Deputy Huff's training and instincts kicked in. Despite the shock of having just been shot, he managed to maneuver to the rear of the driver's car, unholster his pistol, and squeeze off several rounds at the vehicle as it sped away. Miraculously, although the car was struck with multiple rounds, the driver was not hit. As the car disappeared from sight, Deputy Huff used his shoulder-mounted radio to alert the dispatcher, "I've been shot!"[267]

Fortunately for Huff, both bullets had struck him in his bullet-resistant vest. He was badly bruised, but alive.

When police stopped the driver later that night after a brief chase, they were shocked to learn that the driver was only 15-years-old. Why would this young man shoot a police officer on a "routine traffic stop" you might ask? As near as we could tell, he had two reasons. One, he had taken his grandmother's car that night without permission and feared that she would find out if he had been given a traffic ticket. And two, he feared that the deputy would find his 9mm pistol and discover that it had been stolen.

Under ordinary circumstances, this 15-year-old defendant would have been prosecuted in the Juvenile Court where the maximum punishment was just 5 years in a juvenile detention facility. But this was no ordinary case. Had these bullets traveled a few inches to the right or left, Deputy Huff might have been killed that night. So, after weighing the alternatives, I filed a motion to transfer the defendant's case to the Superior Court where the maximum sentence was 20 years confinement. After consulting with both Deputy Huff and the Sheriff, I negotiated a 20-year plea deal that called for the first 12 years to

---

[267] This entire sequence of events was captured on Deputy Huff's dashcam video which I shared with my students.

be served in prison followed by banishment from the Circuit for the remainder of his sentence.[268]

"Routine traffic stops?" There's no such thing.[269]

Crooked Cops

Remember Rodney Benton? He was the alleged drug dealer that I wrote about in Chapter 8 – the one who ate the crack rock. A few years after that episode and his later acquittal on drug sale charges, he was back in jail again awaiting trial on new drug charges. At this point you might be thinking, well, at least while he was being held in jail, he couldn't be dealing drugs. Well, you would be wrong.

The Captain in charge of the jail suspected that Benton was smuggling in drugs and selling them to fellow inmates. Or so he had been told by a jailhouse snitch. So, the Captain directed his jailers to conduct a "shakedown" of Benton's cell block – a thorough search of each cell. When jailers entered the cell block to conduct their search, they observed Benton grab something from under his mattress and attempt to flush it down the toilet in his cell. Before the bowl had emptied, however, one of the jailers was able to fish the object out: a baggie of cocaine.

Already facing drug charges, Benton now faced yet another drug charge: possession of drugs in a penal institution. I decided to try Benton on this new charge first because the evidence was so strong – a conviction was almost assured. There was only one possible hiccup:

---

[268] I had originally planned to recommend a 20-year prison sentence but lowered my plea offer when I discovered that the defendant's mental evaluation may have provided him with a basis for seeking a transfer of the case back to Juvenile Court.

[269] Deputy Huff was the recipient of the "Officer of the Year for Valor" from the Executive Committee of the Peace Officers Association of Georgia in 1997. He was also honored by a Resolution of the Georgia General Assembly. See SR 549 (1/28/98).

We couldn't tell the jury *why* the Captain suspected Benton – that would have involved revealing the snitch's identity.[270] And the Captain couldn't reveal the snitch's statements to him without violating the hearsay rule. So, I met with each of the jailers and gave them the following explicit warning: "When you testify, don't mention the snitch's tip naming Benton."

One of the first jailers to testify, however, almost immediately violated my clear instructions. The testimony sounded something like this:

Cook: Did you participate in the skakedown of Benton's cell block?

Jailer: "Oh, yeah, one of the inmates came forward and said the Benton had some cocaine in his cell, so we...."

Of course, the defense attorney immediately moved for a mistrial which Judge Sorrells granted. I was livid. This was no accident. No slip of the tongue. This was intentional. I went back to my office and fired off an angry letter to the Sheriff insisting that this jailer needed to be investigated for intentionally causing this mistrial. What happened next came totally out of left field.

After receiving my letter, the Sheriff contacted me and told me not to worry, that this jailer would be losing his job soon. It turns out that this jailer was already being investigated for running a prostitution ring! Even more troubling, the Sheriff suspected that this jailer was recruiting female inmates at the jail to use as his prostitutes!

---

[270] The State is entitled to shield the identity of its informants. This not only permits the State to reuse informants in future investigations, it also protects informants against possible retaliation by the persons against whom they snitch.

The Sheriff wanted definitive proof. So, he asked the drug task force to conduct a sting operation. To catch the jailer in the act, the task force met with one of the jailer's suspected prostitutes and persuaded her to lure the jailer to a local motel to "talk business." The task force agents then set up a hidden video camera in one of the motel rooms which they would be able to monitor from an adjoining room. And as expected, the jailer showed up to meet with the cooperating witness and soon uttered the "magic words." Whereupon the cooperating witness opened the door and permitted the task force to enter and arrest the half-dressed, bumfuzzled soon-to-be ex-jailer.[271]

A few months later, I had the pleasure of taking this former jailer's guilty plea.

Abuse of Police Power

In the years immediately preceding the writing of this book, several highly-publicized, yet isolated incidents involving the abuse of police power (and other, subsequently disproven allegations of such abuse) led to a growing mistrust of the police.[272] Often, these incidents were mischaracterized and sensationalized by pseudo-intellectuals, woke politicians, and their media myrmidons. As a result, a false narrative suggesting that such abuses were endemic to policing in America was born.[273] And as the 24-7 news cycle began to focus – sometimes

---

[271] The task force had invited me to join them in the adjacent observation room to monitor the sting operation. Thus, I was able to see the "take-down" live.

[272] For example, the George Floyd case in Minneapolis, Minnesota in May of 2020 was clearly a case of police brutality that led to Floyd's death. But the Michael Brown case in Ferguson, Missouri in August of 2014 clearly was not – as concluded by federal, state, and local authorities. Yet to this day, many in the news media and protest groups continue to lump these two cases into the same category.

[273] This false narrative is discussed and refuted by statistical evidence in Heather MacDonald's book The War on Cops.

obsessively – on each subsequent incident, anger in the affected communities grew to a fever pitch. And despite a spike in the rate of violent crimes in these communities, many called for the "defunding" of police agencies. This anger was further stoked by professional athletes who began to protest the playing of the National Anthem at sporting events. Before long, peaceful protests gave way to violent mobs who attacked police officers, vandalized private property and government buildings, and looted businesses. But perhaps the worst casualty of this societal upheaval was the rule of law itself. As cities burned and statues of American heroes were toppled, feckless governors and mayors just stood back and watched the carnage take place – making no distinction between lawful protests and mob violence.

On the rare occasion when a police officer in my Circuit was accused of on-the-job misconduct, I generally tended to give the officer the benefit of the doubt. Why? Because in my experience, most officers deserved it. Policing is a very difficult job. Often, police officers must make split-second decisions in very hectic, often dangerous circumstances. And like you and me, they want to go home at night to their families safe and sound. So, it seemed to me that a society that hires these men and women – at relatively low pay – and places them in harm's way daily shouldn't be so quick to condemn them when controversy swirls.

Police-Involved Shooting Cases

In my Circuit in the 1990s, I can only recall two incidents where a police officer shot someone in the line of duty – and fortunately, neither person died. On both occasions, however, there was an immediate, knee-jerk reaction calling for the police officers to be charged with a crime.

The "Shot in the Back" Case

In the first incident, a mother and her child were carjacked in an adjoining jurisdiction. Fortunately, they were able to escape unharmed by jumping from the moving vehicle as the perpetrator sped away. Not long afterward, the carjacker was spotted in my Circuit and police gave chase. The carjacker eventually drove off the road into a field toward a stand of trees. His apparent intent was to ditch the car and escape on foot through the woods. But police were hot on his tail and pursued him into the field in their patrol cars. When the carjacker finally brought his car to a stop and attempted to get out of his car, he was almost immediately shot – in the back! As a result of this gunshot wound, he was permanently paralyzed from the waist down.

The carjacker's family was outraged. "The officer shot him in the back," they screamed as they threatened to sue. And the media, smelling a juicy story, asked me incredulously why the officer had not yet been charged. I responded that I intended to wait for the full GBI investigative report before assessing what charges, if any, were called for. "But the officer shot the suspect in the back," the media pleaded, "what else do you need to know?" I found these entreaties, although not unexpected, to be most hypocritical. Did you ever notice how the media – and so-called "community activists" – will criticize a prosecutor for a "rush to judgment" if a charge is brought quickly against an average citizen, but demand a rush to judgment when a police officer or government official is involved?

Fortunately for the officer, his dashcam captured this entire incident on video. The video revealed the following sequence of events: The carjacker and the police officer each stopped their cars at about the same time. Both men got out of their vehicles at about the same time. The carjacker had a long-barreled pistol in his hand and *pointed it at the officer* as he stepped out of his vehicle. The officer, who had unholstered his pistol as he exited his patrol car, aimed his pistol at the gun-wielding suspect and squeezed off a single round at the carjacker. Almost instantaneously, the carjacker spun his body around as he attempted to run toward the woods such that his back was now facing the officer. The bullet struck him in the back. The time elapsed: 1-2 seconds.

When I announced that I would not bring charges against the officer and why, the press seemed satisfied with my explanation although I don't recall being praised for my prudent, wait-and-see attitude. And I can't help but wonder: If there had been no dashcam video, would the media have chosen to believe the officer's account or the carjacker's? I think we know the answer. Which headline would sell more newspapers: "Officer shoots suspect in the back" or "Gun-wielding carjacker captured by police"?

This case illustrates what a big mistake it is for a prosecutor – or the press – to make a snap decision based upon less than all the facts. A prime example being the Michael Brown police shooting case in Ferguson, Missouri in 2014. The news media went ballistic when a police officer shot and killed an unarmed teenager. Riots, looting, and arson soon followed. Yet state and federal investigations determined that the shooting was justified. The officer had only fired when the much larger Brown refused the officer's commands to halt and attempted to attack the officer. (Up to that point, the media had portrayed Brown as a "gentle giant.") The fallout from the media's irresponsible coverage of this incident can still be felt today.

The Lacy Street Shooting Case

The second incident was not so easily resolved.

One night shortly after 2:00am, three Monroe Police officers were conducting a stake-out at a house located on Lacy Street in Monroe, Georgia. Lacy Street was known at that time as "Crack Town" for its street-level drug dealing. The officers were on foot and hiding behind bushes across the street from this house. It was dark and the scene was only dimly illuminated by a streetlamp a half-block away. At some point, the officers noticed two men emerge from this house and start walking in their direction. The officers would later claim that one of these men had apparently caught a glimpse of one of the officers and asked his friend, "Hey, is that the Po-Po?" Translation: Is that the police? The two men would later claim that they didn't know who was hiding in the bushes but suspected that it was an adversary from the community. To flush him out, they claimed that they began throwing rocks at him. What happened next was the subject of a lengthy and controversial investigation by the Georgia Bureau of Investigation (GBI).

One of the officers claimed that instead of throwing rocks at them, one of these two men raised what appeared to be a shiny, chrome object. He then heard what he believed to be the chambering of a round into a semi-automatic pistol. Fearing that a fellow officer was about to be fired upon, he then discharged his weapon in the direction of the two men. Then, a second officer – the one that the first officer believed to be in danger – also began shooting. (Did the officers fire prematurely? Should they have waited until after they were fired upon? Until one of them was shot?) One of the first officer's bullets struck one of the men in the abdomen. The other officer's bullets, however, missed both men and struck the façade of the house across the street. During this hail of bullets, the two men managed to retreat to and re-enter the house behind them. Upon entering the house, the man who was shot collapsed. Meanwhile, the officers fell back to regroup and called for backup. By the time backup arrived, the neighborhood was chaotic.

The wounded man was transported to the hospital. And the chrome-plated pistol that the first officer claimed to have seen and heard was nowhere to be found. (Did the officer actually see a pistol? Did he actually hear a round being chambered? Did someone take the pistol from the scene to enable the two men to claim that they had been unarmed?) Two days later, the wounded man, Romeo Carr, was released from the hospital. And the media firestorm commenced.

So, why were the officers on Lacy Street that night? The officers claimed that they had seen a man with outstanding arrest warrants enter Carr's residence and that they were waiting for him to leave so they could safely arrest him outside the house. Carr, on the other hand, as well as the second man, Cedrick Wymbs – and their Atlanta attorney who later threatened to file a $10 million lawsuit against the City of Monroe – claimed that the presence of the police officers on Lacy Street that night was harassment, pure and simple. Moreover, they claimed that neither Carr nor Wymbs had a pistol that night. Instead, they claimed that what the officer saw and heard was a pair of shiny sunglasses that made a "click-clack" sound when Wymbs removed it and placed it in his shirt pocket. (Would someone really be fiddling with a pair of sunglasses at 2:00am in the pitch-black darkness?) The Chief of Police and Mayor quickly came to the officers' defense. (Why would their officers intentionally shoot an unarmed man who posed no threat?)

All three officers were placed on routine administrative leave and the GBI was called in to investigate. A background check of Carr and Wymbs revealed that both had prior weapons-related charges. (Thus, lending credence to the first officer's claim that he had seen a weapon.) Each officer was then separately questioned by GBI Agent Mike Pearson, but no new information was revealed. Afterward, however, a witness stepped forward that would undermine the credibility of the officers' account of the shooting. A local high school student contacted the GBI several weeks after the incident to report that he had been present on Lacy Street that night. In fact, he had been with the three officers that night doing a ride-along as part of a Boy Scout sponsored "explorer scout" program. (Why hadn't the officers mentioned this explorer scout in their statements to the GBI? What were the officers attempting to cover up?)

When confronted with this teenager's claim, the officers conceded that they had failed to mention this explorer scout's presence with them that night when first questioned by the GBI. The officers claimed, however, that they had no intention of misleading the GBI regarding the shooting incident itself. Instead, their intent was to conceal the fact that they had violated a Monroe Police Department policy that prohibited officers from permitting explorer scouts to get out of their patrol cars during potentially dangerous encounters. Nonetheless, upon learning that his officers had not been totally forthcoming with the GBI, the Chief of Police immediately fired all three of the officers.

When I received the GBI's investigative report (which, incidentally, reached no conclusion regarding the officers' criminal liability in the shooting of Romeo Carr), and after personally interviewing the explorer scout, I announced my intention to convene a grand jury investigation into the shooting incident. I drafted indictments against Carr, Wymbs, *and* all three of the officers. It was my intention to give the grand jury every possible option. I drafted indictments charging Carr and Wymbs with Aggravated Assault[274] and charging two of the officers with Aggravated Assault and all three with Giving False Statements (to a GBI Agent). This would enable the grand jury

---

[274] I drafted indictments against both men because the officers never definitively identified which of the two men allegedly held the shiny pistol.

to indict Carr, Wymbs, or the officers – *if* they believed that there was probable cause to do so.

When the grand jury met in January of 2000, I presented the testimony of more than a dozen witnesses over 2 days.[275] GBI Agent Mike Pearson testified at length regarding his investigation. Among other things, he described Lacy Street and its reputation for lawlessness. He described the scene of the shooting itself using an aerial photograph that had been taken from a GBI helicopter. (The GBI had truly spared no expense on this one.) He also detailed the relevant weapon-related criminal histories of both Carr and Wymbs and revealed that a witness had come forward to say that Wymbs in fact owned a chrome-plated pistol. (Was that the object that the first officer claimed to have seen and heard?) To distinguish between a "good shoot" and a "bad shoot," I called a firearms expert from the Georgia Police Academy to explain what police recruits are taught about the use of deadly force. (As I recall, this expert concluded that the officers likely fired their weapons prematurely but that such judgment calls must be made instantaneously without the benefit of hindsight.)

When the explorer scout testified, he told the grand jury that the officers had instructed him not to tell anyone that he had been present at the shooting scene. (That must have moved the grand jurors to the edge of their seats.) But he also testified that he was hiding behind a tree at the time of the shooting and didn't see what, if anything, Carr and Wymbs had in their hands at that time of the shooting. (Likely resulting in the grand jurors sitting back in their chairs.) Moreover, he testified that one officer yelled, "Don't do it. Don't do it. Put it down," before the first shot was fired. (Suggesting that this officer thought – rightly or wrongly – that he saw a gun.)

---

[275] See Olsen v. State, 302 Ga. 288 (2017)(discussing the scope of grand jury secrecy).

And finally, Carr, Wymbs, and the three officers were all given their chance to address the grand jury.

Although it was clear to me that the explorer scout's testimony had done absolutely nothing to assist the grand jury in its "good shoot – bad shoot" analysis, the fact that the officers had attempted to conceal the explorer scout's identity as a "possible" witness had not only hampered the investigation, it had damaged the credibility of the officers – and the Monroe Police Department. I thought at the time that the grand jury would probably "no bill" all of the Aggravated Assault charges but "true bill" the False Statements charges against all three officers. The grand jury, however, declined to return *any* indictments against *any* of the players in this controversial case.[276]

* * *

I have heard people criticize the grand jury system when a grand jury fails to indict someone in a high-profile case (like the Lacy Street Shooting Case or the Ferguson, Missouri case). These critics often complain that the grand jury in such cases (or more often, the prosecutor who presented the case to the grand jury) deprived the community of a "public trial." But this criticism misses the mark. It misperceives *who* the grand jurors are and the important *role* that they play in our system of criminal justice.

The grand jury is composed of twenty-three *citizens* – all of whom are randomly selected from the community where the crime

---

[276] A civil lawsuit against the three police officers was dismissed on the basis of the officers' qualified immunity. Carr v. Tatangelo, Case No. 01-14621 (11th Cir. 2003)(holding that "[w]hile the officers may not have exhibited paradigmatic police work in … the early morning hours in question, Carr and Wymbs have failed to state constitutional violations or show that the officers' conduct was unreasonable under clearly established law on the objective facts of this case that would render the officers liable for damages").

was committed. Grand jurors are instructed that they may issue a "true bill" of indictment if they determine that the evidence presented establishes *probable cause* to believe that the accused person is guilty of the crime charged. In other words, if there is a *fair probability* that such person committed it. This is a low standard of proof. Moreover, this determination doesn't even require unanimity. In fact, it only requires a *simple majority vote*, i.e., the votes of only 12 (or more) of the 23 grand jurors. Thus, when a grand jury declines to issue an indictment in a case, it is an indication that a majority of the grand jurors believed that probable cause was lacking (or otherwise believed that prosecution of the accused person was not warranted).

So, one must ask: If fewer than half of the members of a grand jury believe that there is probable cause to justify the issuance of an indictment in a given case, how likely is it that a jury of 12 citizens (drawn from the *same* community as the grand jurors) at a "public trial" would *unanimously* find the defendant in that case guilty *beyond a reasonable doubt?* This question, if answered honestly, reveals the true role of the grand jury in our system of criminal justice: It acts as a safeguard against "show trials" – trials that may boost a prosecutor's political aspirations, or sate the media's desire for a juicy story, or quench the public's thirst for melodrama, but do little to achieve justice or safeguard the rights of the wrongfully accused.

Nonetheless, in cases involving alleged criminal misconduct by law enforcement officers, I have long advocated that a prosecutor[277] from another Circuit should be appointed to handle such cases. This

---

[277] Some have suggested the appointment of a "special prosecutor." I reject this proposal because I fear that the appointing authority might be tempted to select a lawyer without any prosecutorial training or experience – someone lacking objectivity and with an anti-police agenda who might attempt to appease those in the media or in the community by indicting a weak case.

would remove any possibility that the grand jury proceeding might be unduly influenced by the bias or prejudice of the local District Attorney – for or against the officer. It would also protect a local District Attorney from the risk of losing the good will of the local law enforcement community should he or she be forced to prosecute one of its popular members. [278]

---

[278] Although I think that there's truth in the saying that "no one hates a bad cop as much as a good cop."

CHAPTER 14

The Halls of Justice

I have no problem with state and federal courthouses that are majestic in their appearance and extravagant in their cost. Why? Because when people enter *their* courthouses, I think they should be awed and humbled. They should immediately realize that they are not just standing in a fancy building adorned with marble and mahogany, they are in a place where the rule of law lives and justice may be sought and attained – a place that serves as the very embodiment of the ideals expressed in the Declaration of Independence, the United States Constitution, and the Bill of Rights.

When United States Supreme Court Justice Anthony Kennedy came to Covington, Georgia, to dedicate the new Newton County Judicial Center in 1999,[279] he said this about courthouses:

> To build this structure reconfirms the principle that the [American] people rule themselves. That principle is not inherited, it is not genetic. It has to be taught to each generation and

---

[279] This was a most unusual event. It was reportedly the first dedication of a rural courthouse by a sitting Supreme Court Justice. Rumor has it that Judge Samuel Ozburn had made numerous entreaties to Justice Kennedy before finally "wearing him down." Before the dedication ceremony, my wife and I were privileged to share a meal with Justice Kennedy along with other public officials at an old manor house in Covington.

transferred from one age to the next. This courthouse stands for the biggest idea in the history of the American republic. The law deals with the abstract, the general, with ideas. It deals with intangibles. So, when we have the opportunity to see something tangible, something real, something concrete, as a representation of the law, it's a reason to celebrate.

When I first became District Attorney in 1990, the two DA's Offices in the Alcovy Circuit were located in the Walton County Courthouse constructed in 1883 and the Newton County Courthouse constructed in 1884. Both courthouses were designed by the same architect, and although they bore similar features, each was unique in its own way. Unfortunately, both courthouses had seen better days and were in bad need of a major overhaul.

The Walton County Courthouse

I was particularly fond of the Walton County Courthouse (a photo of which is shown on the front cover and spine of this book). In 1985, I got my start in the Alcovy Circuit when I was hired by Chief Judge Thomas Ridgeway to serve as his judicial law clerk. I had a great office nestled in the building's roof overlooking the front lawn. It was a quiet place to research and draft the judge's civil orders – although I would occasionally be interrupted by squirrels or birds chasing one another on the ceiling tiles above my head. When I became an ADA, my office was again on the top floor, but this time on the backside of the building. And finally, when I became District Attorney, I moved to a more spacious office on the second floor with a picturesque view of the front lawn and downtown Monroe.

The main courtroom – actually, the only courtroom – though quite functional, was rather drab. Try to visualize olive green carpet adjacent to peel 'n' stick red and black tiles, a suspended tile ceiling with fluorescent light fixtures, and faded grey paneling. Now imagine each of those features being decades old. Fortunately, early into my tenure, a 2.5 million-dollar SPLOST (special local option sales tax) was passed to restore the Walton County Courthouse to its 19th-century grandeur. In the meantime, however, the District Attorney's Office, the judge's chambers, the Clerk's Office, and the courtroom would have to be moved. But where?

The 1990s saw Walmart chase many downtown retailers out of business. Adcock's Department Store located directly across Broad Street from the old courthouse was one of these businesses. And that is where we moved. It was somewhat comical to prosecute criminal cases in a building that once sold menswear and ladies' shoes. But this new space actually served us well for many years. And, frankly, it was more spacious and utilitarian than our old courthouse digs.

When the old courthouse renovation project was complete, it was a showplace. So much so that Judge Sorrells decided that it was too grand to countenance the presence of criminals. He simply could not bear the thought of prisoners scarring the new oak banisters and hardwood floors with their leg and waist chains. So, we continued to hold criminal court in the Courthouse Annex until a new Walton County Courthouse was built on the outskirts of town – years after my tenure as District Attorney had ended.

Although the Courthouse Annex proved to be more than adequate for our criminal arraignments and trials, there was one design flaw that almost led to the reversal of a death sentence. Following the trial of Brian "Chico" Terrell,[280] attorney John Strauss filed a motion for new trial in which he claimed that the jury room was not properly

---

[280] See Chapter 10 – Death Penalty Cases, The Brian "Chico" Terrell Case.

sound-proofed. Strauss alleged that jurors *may* have overheard sensitive motion hearings taking place in the courtroom while the jurors were taking breaks in the adjacent jury room. To support this hypothesis, Strauss directed his investigators to conduct an experiment in the courtroom. As it was later revealed, this "experiment" consisted of one private investigator shouting from the witness stand while another pressed his ear against the door of the jury room. The latter investigator claimed to have heard the former investigator's shouts quite clearly.

Of course, this experiment was hardly scientific. Nonetheless, I knew that given the hypersensitive scrutiny given to all claims of error in death penalty cases, I could not afford to take Strauss' hypothesis lightly. I knew that I would have to thoroughly debunk this theory to preserve Terrell's death sentence on appeal. So, what did I, a proud graduate of the University of Georgia, do? I hired an audiologist with a Ph.D. from Georgia's arch-rival, the Georgia Institute of Technology (a.k.a. Georgia Tech)! Using sophisticated machinery, this expert determined that even if a juror had been standing at the door of the jury room, he or she would only have been able to make out every third word spoken from the witness stand and would not have been able to make any coherent sense out of what was heard. Strauss' motion was denied.

The Newton County Courthouse

I rarely had the opportunity to visit the Newton County Courthouse until after I was elected District Attorney. At that point, however, I needed to have an office there as well as in Walton County. In fact, I made the decision early on to split my time as evenly as possible between the two courthouses – after all, I had been elected as the District Attorney for *both* counties.[281]

There were several quirky things about the District Attorney's Office located on the basement floor of the Newton County Courthouse. One, there were at least seven unguarded ways to enter our office – four exterior entrances and three interior entrances. That would never pass muster in our more security-minded courthouses today. Two, our offices were a maze of hallways that stretched from one corner of the building to the other – with the public restrooms located in the center. Several of my ADAs and staffers literally had their desks in hallways with no privacy walls or doors. And our evidence locker was located under a publicly accessible staircase leading to the public restrooms. Thus, any junkie with a screwdriver could have easily stolen our drug evidence. And my investigators' offices flooded every time that it rained. I think about that office every time I hear a public defender bemoan the "limitless resources of the State."

The Newton County Courthouse underwent several renovations in the 1990s. During these renovations, we were sometimes forced to conduct trials and arraignments in several temporary quarters located outside the Courthouse. The first was the second floor of the old Belk's Department Store building. A distinctive feature of this makeshift courtroom was a support column located right slap dab in the middle of the front of the courtroom. Counsel had to slide their chairs to the right or left to make eye contact with the judge on the bench or the witness on the witness stand! The second was the old Patrick's Feed-N-Seed building – which made Adcock's Department Store in

---

[281] Sheriff Franklin Thornton in Walton County, who was a fine Sheriff and a great mentor to me in my fledgling District Attorney career, was particularly jealous of the time I spent in Newton County. I'm not sure he ever believed me when I told him that I spent 2 ½ days in each county each week. But I really did.

Walton County look like the New York Museum of Natural History by comparison.

And even when we did have access to the courtroom in the Newton County Courthouse, things did not always go according to plans. On one occasion, we were trying a case when the trial was interrupted by loud hammering coming from the roof. The judge dispatched a bailiff to find out what was going on. Apparently, a roofing contractor had been instructed by the County Commission to perform repairs on the roof. The judge, who was not pleased, summoned the contractor to the courtroom and cautioned him that if he heard one more hammer strike, he would be held in contempt of court.

And we often had to make special accommodations for disabled persons because the Courthouse did not have an elevator. Once, we had to hold a bond hearing for a wheelchair-bound woman[282] on the ground floor of the Courthouse in a hallway outside the public restrooms. Halls of justice indeed!

Eventually, the Newton County Commission decided that it needed to build a new courthouse. And in 1999, the new Newton County Judicial Center, located behind the historic 1884 Courthouse, was dedicated by United States Supreme Court Justice Anthony M. Kennedy. I was fortunate to work in the new Judicial Center for several years before retiring from active prosecution in 2001.[283]

---

[282] This woman – the matriarch of a drug-dealing family – weighed over 300 lbs. So, there was no way to carry her up the stairs to the main courtroom.

[283] In 2020, following the untimely death of Superior Court Judge Horace J. Johnson, Jr., the Judicial Center was re-named the Horace J. Johnson, Jr. Judicial Center – a fitting honor for this outstanding public servant and native of Newton County.

CHAPTER 15

A Team Approach

A district attorney is like the player-manager of a baseball team.[284] A player-manager not only manages his team, but he may also insert himself into the starting lineup and play the game. Similarly, a district attorney not only supervises a staff of ADAs who are responsible for handling the office's caseload, but he or she may also select certain cases to prosecute himself or herself. I relished both of these roles during my tenure as District Attorney.

Many who assume the title "District Attorney" choose to trade their status as a trial lawyer for that of an office administrator. I was not one of them. Even after my move from ADA to DA, I wanted to be in the courtroom trying cases. In other words, I wanted to be "in the game." If anything, I tried *more* cases per year as District Attorney than I did as an ADA. My chosen caseload consisted primarily of murder cases, politically-sensitive cases, and special victim cases. But that still left the lion's share of the cases to be tried by the other prosecutors in my office. And whereas I relied upon these ADAs to try these cases, they relied upon our staffers to assist them in getting their cases ready for trial. This highlights the fact that no district attorney can expect

---

[284] Famous player-managers in Major League Baseball include Frank Robinson and Pete Rose.

to enjoy success without a stable of competent ADAs and a dedicated supporting staff.

Fortunately, I inherited a talented team of staffers when I first assumed office – experienced administrative assistants, secretaries, and DA investigators. All that remained was the equally important task of recruiting a strong core of assistant district attorneys. Because the starting salary for an ADA in my rural Circuit was abysmally low, almost all of my ADA hires were young, recent law school graduates with little or no experience. But what they lacked in experience, they more than made up for in enthusiasm. And I truly enjoyed training them up and watching them evolve into top-flight prosecutors.

Although I started with just two ADAs, by the time my tenure in office ended, I had a total of nine ADAs. Many of these ADAs stayed with me for several years. Unfortunately, I lost more than a few to higher-paying jobs in Metro Atlanta. As a result, I rarely had more than a few experienced ADAs at any given time. Nonetheless, my ADAs and I persevered and survived the slings and arrows endemic to our profession.

It was truly "a team approach."

The Line Prosecutors

The vast majority of the prosecutorial work done in a District Attorney's Office is performed by the "line prosecutors." These are the assistant district attorneys on the front lines in the processing of thousands of cases each year. Week in and week out, the line prosecutors are the ones who review the new cases, handle the bond and preliminary hearings, screen out the weak and frivolous cases, draft the accusations and indictments, present the felony cases to the grand jury, negotiate the plea agreements, furnish the discovery material, present the guilty pleas and accept the not guilty pleas, handle the pretrial motion hearings, and try cases.

I have often described the line prosecutor's job as the equivalent of that of an air traffic controller. An ADA must keep a constant eye on his or her "radar screen" of pending cases – trying to keep each one on a steady "flight path" to its final destination: a guilty plea, a trial, an appeal, or a dismissal. But an ADA's job, like that of an air traffic controller, is never done. Because for every case an ADA resolves, there's another case about to "take off."

Over the years, I had the good fortune of hiring some extraordinarily talented line prosecutors. Ken Wynne was my Chief ADA from the very beginning and stayed with me for my entire tenure as District Attorney. He was a solid partner and a damn good trial lawyer. Together, we made a formidable team. For 10 years, we were the lead trial attorneys who handled the office's most serious and controversial cases. And when I decided to step aside, Ken was the obvious choice to take my place as the next District Attorney in 2001.[285]

As mentioned above, it was hard to attract, hire, and keep experienced lawyers in the Alcovy Circuit. As a result, I hired almost all of my ADAs straight out of law school. These young ADAs were eager, idealistic, and excited about starting their legal careers as prosecutors. A few even stayed with me beyond their initial two-year commitments.

---

[285] We nicknamed Wynne "the Bulldog" because of his tenacity. Among his many impressive trial victories was a death penalty case involving a man accused of burning his three young children in a trailer home. In another, I watched Ken as he enticed a murder defendant to come down from the witness stand and demonstrate how he shot a man in the back of the head – all the while maintaining that he had done so in self-defense.

Among these were: Anne Templeton LaMalva,[286] Jeff Foster,[287] Jay Jackson,[288] and Brian Deutsch[289] in Walton County; and Jennifer Greene Ammons,[290] Jeff Blandford,[291] and Chris Brasher[292] in Newton County. Two other ADAs deserve special mention. Vanessa Webber, who served as our circuit-wide juvenile prosecutor, joined our office in the mid-1990s and is still there as of the writing of this book. And Layla Zon,[293] my last ADA hire, later succeeded Ken Wynne as District Attorney in 2010.

---

[286] Among LaMalva's many accomplishments as a prosecutor, she tried our office's first successful "Two Strikes" case involving a serial rapist. She once received a certificate of "Eptness" from her lawyer-husband after a judge questioned her trial tactics – despite having won her case. Anne would later become the Circuit's Child Support Recovery lawyer.

[287] The only Blue Hen from the University of Delaware that I've ever met, Foster once accompanied police to a murder scene and found the murder weapon where it had been hidden under a footbridge. Jeff would later establish a successful private practice in Monroe and serve as a Municipal Court Judge before his election to the Alcovy Superior Court bench in 2020.

[288] Having grown up around cattle, Jackson was the only one of my ADAs who could schmooze with the farmers on the jury panel about their Charolais, Herefords, and Holsteins. Jay would go on to have a successful career as a prosecutor in Clayton County.

[289] Deutsch, nicknamed "Hootie," was a swimmer as an undergraduate at UGA and later became a successful civil litigator in Atlanta after a stint with the Georgia Attorney General's Office.

[290] Among Ammon's more interesting cases was her successful prosecution of a vehicular homicide case in which the defendant raised a "narcolepsy" defense. She also orchestrated an "arson dog" demonstration in the courtroom once that prompted defense counsel to concede, "That's one smart dog." Jennifer would later serve as General Counsel for the Georgia Dept. of Driver Services and the Georgia Dept. of Corrections.

[291] Blandford probably took the most memorable guilty plea in my 10 years in office – a "Criminal Attempt to Commit Cruelty to Animals" case. As Forrest Gump would say, "That's all I have to say about that."

[292] Brasher was a human thesaurus – he had the most impressive vocabulary of anyone I've ever known. Chris would later join the State Attorney General's Office before his appointment to the Fulton Superior Court bench in 2006.

[293] Zon quickly became one of the State's finest trial attorneys. After serving as DA for 10 years, Layla was appointed to the Alcovy Superior Court bench in 2020.

Although many of my other ADA hires did not stay as long as the ones mentioned above – most leaving to pursue higher-paying jobs elsewhere – they nonetheless made valuable contributions to the success of our two offices. They included: Eric Morrow, Mary Diversi Hanks, Jenny Parker, Gene Hatcher, Cassandra Kirk, Len Myers, Brian Frost, Brian Max, Sean Dolan, Melanie Biondi, Mary Beth Murphy, and Greg Wagner.

Together, in addition to our many other accomplishments (which included resolving thousands of cases *without* a trial), my ADAs and I compiled a very impressive record of trial victories. These trial statistics are summarized in the chart at the end of this chapter. All told, we had a jury trial success rate of 82.1%. The acquittal rate was just 11.2%. And a 6.7% mistrial rate accounted for the rest. These ADAs served their communities with honor and distinction – and made me look good in the process. I will be forever grateful for their loyalty to me and their dedicated service to the citizens of the Alcovy Judicial Circuit.

The DA's Staff

None of the accomplishments listed in the preceding section could have been achieved if it had not been for the able assistance of our DA staff consisting of administrative assistants, secretaries, DA investigators, and victim advocates. Brenda Hitchcock, the lead administrative assistant in the Newton office, and Donna Fambrough, the lead administrative assistant in the Walton office, were not only the most important cogs in managing these two offices, but they were also my sounding boards, my voices of reason - the ones who I could go to share my thoughts – and frustrations.[294] Their support and sage advice were invaluable. Playing equally important support roles were Jan

---

[294] At particularly stressful times, Brenda and I would jokingly discuss quitting our jobs and opening up a donut shop together. Donna, on the other hand, a high school sports standout, never

McGaughey, Melanie Sims, and Debbie Greer in Walton County and Kathy Kitchens, Cindi Malcom, and Leslie Smith in Newton County. These eight women were the heart and soul of these offices in the 1990s.

My investigators Herman Bradford,[295] Otis Harper, and Mike Burke[296] – all former law enforcement officers – helped maintain good working relations with the law enforcement agencies in the Circuit. They made sure that we received all of the materials that we need to successfully prosecute our cases: police reports, crime lab reports, Georgia Crime Information Center printouts, and certified copies. They also served our witness subpoenas and ensured that these sometimes elusive witnesses were present to testify at court hearings and trials. My victim advocates Lori Woods and Joe Rickman[297] kept crime victims and their families apprised of the progress of their cases. They also assisted victims in receiving the services and compensation to which they were entitled. As with my ADAs, I will be forever grateful for these staff members' loyalty to me and their dedicated service to the citizens of the Alcovy Judicial Circuit.

---

seemed to let anything get her down. She was one of the few people I knew who could handle the temperamental personalities in the courthouse without batting an eye.

[295] Bradford served the DA's Office faithfully throughout my 14-year career as a prosecutor. His wife, Maggie, was secretary to the Newton judges and was a joy to work with.

[296] Burke was a talented officer and investigator who I hired away from the Monroe PD. Mike would later become the Chief Magistrate Judge in Walton County.

[297] Rickman, a former deputy sheriff, also performed many investigative duties for my office. Joe was always full of energy. We joked that he probably consumed his coffee from an IV drip. Joe later joined the Fulton DA's Office as an investigator before becoming the Chief Investigator for the Fulton County PD's Office.

ALCOVY JUDICIAL CIRCUIT JURY TRIALS (1991-2000)

NEWTON COUNTY

No. of Jury Trials	212
Guilty Verdicts	133
Guilty Pleas[298]	43
Not Guilty Verdicts	24
Mistrials	12

WALTON COUNTY

No. of Jury Trials	162
Guilty Verdicts	95
Guilty Pleas	36
Not Guilty Verdicts	18
Mistrials	13

NEWTON & WALTON COUNTIES

No. of Jury Trials[299]	374
Guilty Verdicts	228
Guilty Pleas	79
Not Guilty Verdicts	42
Mistrials	25

---

[298] If a defendant forced us to select a jury and then chose to plead guilty before the jury reached a verdict in the case, I counted that as a "jury trial." We had done the hard work of preparing that case for trial and, but for that hard work, the defendant would not have pled guilty.

[299] My chief assistant Ken Wynne and I were the only two prosecutors who tried cases in each of the 10 years that I served as District Attorney. I tried 98 cases and he tried 85 during these 10 years. Others who tried a significant proportion of these cases included: Jennifer Ammons (35), Anne LaMalva (28), Jeff Foster (21), Jeff Blandford (20), Jay Jackson (19), Chris Brasher (16), and Brian Deutsch (12).

EPILOGUE

I loved being a prosecutor. The trappings of political office – not so much. But I did enjoy the non-political aspects of being the Circuit's lead prosecutor – including the inherent power to make policy and to set priorities. It was truly a job where one person could make a difference.

I took great pride in preparing my cases for trial – some might say to the point of obsession. I always tried to out-prepare opposing counsel. This involved knowing my case facts, my theory of the case, and the legal principles that governed the law of the case. And I'd like to think that my well-organized presentations of the evidence and my personal sincerity more than compensated for my lack of grandiloquence. Partial affirmation of this - and one of my most prized possessions – is a framed letter that I received upon my retirement from active prosecution from the Criminal Investigation Division (CID) of the Newton County Sheriff's Office. The text of this letter reads as follows:

Letter of Appreciation

July 20, 2001

Dear Mr. Cook,

We are all joining together to say congratulations to you on your new teaching position at the University of Georgia. You have been an outstanding District Attorney for Newton County and the Alcovy Judicial Circuit and you will be greatly missed.

It was always a pleasure to watch you in action in the courtroom. The time you spent in preparation, researching and organizing cases was plainly visible. Your case win percentages reflect your legal skills, but it is your deeper qualities that won the respect of so many seasoned investigators.

Truth, honor and justice are more than just words; they represent ideals that are worth fighting for and it has been a pleasure to work with a prosecutor who reflects those values so clearly.

Finally, I would be remiss if I didn't mention the contributions and sacrifices of my family, my wonderful wife, Debra, and son, Philip. No public official with a family does the job alone. We are often forced to work late hours and weekends at the office, and even when home, our minds are often preoccupied with office-related concerns. I will be forever grateful that I had a wife and son who kept me grounded, gave me a place where I could escape the pressures of my job, and gave me the strength to carry on.

APPENDIX A

Jury Trials
(Complete List)

1988

1. State v. Williams (Walton County / drug sale / guilty verdict)
2. State v. Akery (Walton County / speeding / not guilty verdict)
3. State v. Moon (Walton County / speeding / guilty verdict)
4. State v. Wright (Walton County / pointing pistol / not guilty verdict)
5. State v. Martin (Walton County / DUI / not guilty verdict)

1989

6. State v. Huggins (Walton County / child molestation / guilty verdict)
7. State v. Hardge (Walton Count / drug sale / guilty verdict)
8. State v. Roberts (Walton County / drug sale / guilty verdict)
9. State v. Adams (Newton County / drug sale / guilty verdict)
10. State v. Wise (Newton County / drug sale / guilty verdict)
11. State v. Sims (Walton County / child molestation / guilty verdict)

1990

12. State v. Vinson (Walton County / armed robbery / guilty verdict)
13. State v. Robertson (Walton County / aggravated assault / guilty verdict)
14. State v. Ross (Walton County / burglary / guilty verdict)
15. State v. Floyd (Walton County / drug sale / guilty verdict)
16. State v. Fox (Newton County / drug sale / guilty verdict)
17. State v. Taggart (Walton County / child molestation / guilty plea before verdict)

1991

18. State v. Crawford (Walton County / possession w/intent to distribute / guilty verdict)
19. State v. Martin (Walton County / murder / guilty verdict)
20. State v. Benton (Newton County / murder / not guilty)
21. State v. Hardy (Newton County / possession w/intent to distribute / guilty plea to lesser offense before verdict)
22. State v. Orouk (Newton County / sale of alcohol to minor / guilty verdict)
23. State v. Starnes (Walton County / child molestation / guilty verdict)
24. State v. Weaver (Newton County / murder / guilty plea before verdict)
25. State v. Johnson (Walton County / murder / guilty verdict)
26. State v. Capps (Newton County / child molestation / guilty plea before verdict)
27. State v. Nix (Newton County / vehicular homicide / guilty verdict)

28. State v. Hester (Walton County / possession w/intent to distribute / not guilty verdict)

1992

29. State v. Valenti (Newton County / vol. manslaughter / guilty verdict)
30. State v. Atkinson (Walton County / child molestation / guilty plea before verdict)
31. State v. Day (Newton County / child molestation / guilty plea to lesser offense before verdict)
32. State v. Rutledge (Walton County / invol. manslaughter / guilty verdict)
33. State v. Taylor (Walton County / burglary / guilty verdict)
34. State v. Cosby (Newton County / drug sale / mistrial)
35. State v. Benton (Newton County / drug sale / not guilty verdict)
36. State v. Norton (Newton County / murder / guilty verdict)
37. State v. Walker (Newton County / murder / not guilty verdict)

1993

38. State v. Baynes (Newton County / drug sale / guilty plea before verdict)
39. State v. Mathis (Newton County / armed robbery / guilty verdict)
40. State v. Ramming (Walton County / speeding / guilty verdict)
41. State v. Cost, A and Cost, B. (Walton County / murder / guilty verdicts)
42. State v. Thompson (Walton County / habitual violator & DUI / guilty verdict)

43. State v. Zankli (Newton County / theft by deception / guilty plea before verdict)
44. State v. Jones (Newton County / child molestation / guilty verdict)
45. State v. Smith (Newton County / vehicular homicide / not guilty verdict)
46. State v. Shepherd (Newton County / child molestation / guilty verdict)
47. State v. Mitchell (Newton County / child molestation / not guilty verdict)
48. State v. Benton (Newton County / possession w/intent to distribute / mistrial)

1994

49. State v. Fincher (Newton County / child molestation / guilty verdict)
50. State v. Jackson (Walton County / drug sale / guilty verdict)
51. State v. Anglin (Newton County / DUI / guilty verdict)
52. State v. McNight (Newton County / drug sale / guilty verdict)
53. State v. Pickett (Newton County / child molestation / guilty plea before verdict)
54. State v. Grier (Newton County / drug possession / guilty verdict)
55. State v. Durham (Walton County / drug sale / guilty verdict)
56. State v. Terrell (Newton County / murder / mistrial)
57. State v. Charpentier (Newton County / child molestation / guilty verdict)
58. State v. Campbell and Reid (Newton County / armed robbery / guilty verdicts)

59. State v. Price (Newton County / drug sale / guilty plea before verdict)

60. State v. Jackson (Walton County / drug sale / guilty verdict)

1995

61. State v. Terrell (Newton County / murder / guilty verdict / death penalty)

62. State v. Cotner (Walton County / child molestation / not guilty verdict)

63. State v. Holloway (Walton County / child molestation / mistrial)

64. State v. Campbell (Newton Count / child molestation / guilty verdict)

65. State v. Tinker (Walton County / RICO & burglary / guilty verdict)

66. State v. Edwards (Walton County / obstruction of officer & DUI / guilty verdict)

67. State v. Wise (Newton County / drug sale / guilty verdict)

68. State v. Aaron (Newton County / rape & child molestation / not guilty verdict)

69. State v. Stinson (Newton County / armed robbery / guilty verdict)

70. State v. Roebuck (Walton County / child molestation / guilty verdict)

71. State v. Hardge (Walton County / drug sale / mistrial)

72. State v. Neal and Gober (Walton County / drug sale / not guilty verdicts)

1996

73. State v. McGarity (Newton County / child molestation / guilty verdict)

74. State v. Parham (Walton County / solicitation to commit murder / guilty verdict)

75. State v. Wilson (Walton County / reckless conduct / not guilty verdict)

76. State v. Young (Walton County / junk car ordinance / guilty plea before verdict)

77. State v. Smith (Walton County / aggravated sodomy / guilty verdict)

78. State v. Moody, Anderson, and Davis (Newton County / armed robbery / guilty verdicts)

79. State v. Moon (Walton County / speeding / guilty verdict)

80. State v. Glover (Newton County / aggravated assault / guilty plea before verdict)

81. State v. Clay (Walton County / armed robbery / guilty verdict)

82. State v. Morrell (Walton County / theft by receiving & possession w/intent to distribute / guilty verdict)

83. State v. Ramey (Newton County / kidnapping & armed robbery / guilty verdict)

1997

84. State v. Peters (Newton County / child molestation / guilty plea before verdict)

85. State v. Morris (Newton County / child molestation / guilty verdict)

86. State v. Davis (Newton County / murder & aggravated assault / guilty verdict on lesser offense)

87. State v. Walsh (Walton Count / child molestation / guilty verdict)

88. State v. McCallie (Newton County / child molestation / mistrial)
89. State v. Bracewell (Walton County / vol. manslaughter / guilty verdict)
90. State v. Brown (Newton County / murder & armed robbery / guilty verdict)

1998

91. State v. Walker (Newton County / child molestation / guilty verdict)
92. State v. Davis (Newton County / aggravated assault / guilty plea before verdict)
93. State v. Blake (Newton County / theft by taking / guilty plea before verdict)
94. State v. Nolley (Newton County / DUI / guilty plea before verdict)
95. State v. Davis (Newton County / entering auto / guilty plea before verdict)
96. State v. Hamby (Newton County / arson / guilty plea before verdict)
97. State v. Palmer (Walton County / child molestation / guilty plea before verdict)
98. State v. Hughes (Walton County / child molestation / guilty verdict)
99. State v. McCallie (Newton County / child molestation / not guilty verdict)
100. State v. Berry (Newton County / DUI / not guilty verdict)
101. State v. Schoolcraft (Newton County / child molestation / mistrial)

1999

102. State v. George (Newton County / murder / guilty plea before verdict)

103. State v. Roseberry (Newton County / murder & armed robbery / guilty verdict)

104. State v. George (Walton County / attempted extortion / not guilty verdict)

105. State v. Freeman (Walton County / child molestation / guilty verdict)

106. State v. Croy (Walton County / child molestation / guilty verdict)

107. State v. Griffith (Walton County / obstruction of an officer / guilty verdict)

108. State v. Manuel (Newton County / murder & armed robbery / guilty verdict)

2000

109. State v. Posey (Walton County / child molestation / guilty verdict)

110. State v. Meadows (Walton County / sexual battery / guilty verdict)

111. State v. Thurman (Newton County / child molestation / guilty verdict)

112. State v. Durden (Walton County / murder / guilty verdict)

113. State v. Horner (Newton County /motor vehicle theft / guilty verdict)

114. State v. Benton (Newton County / possession w/intent to distribute / guilty plea before verdict)

115. State v. Phelps (Walton County / murder / guilty verdict)

2001

116. State v. Terrell (Newton County / murder / guilty verdict / death penalty)
117. State v. Walker (Newton County / child molestation / guilty verdict)
118. State v. Simmons (Newton County / aggravated assault / guilty verdict)
119. State v. Sparks (Newton County / murder / guilty verdict)
120. State v. Bridges (Newton County / escape / guilty verdict)
121. State v. Raines (Newton County / child molestation / mistrial)
122. State v. Carroll (Walton County / sexual exploitation of minor / guilty plea before verdict)

APPENDIX B

Appellate Cases
(Complete List)
[Affirmed Unless Otherwise Indicated]
[*Cases Orally Argued]

1989

1. Huggins v. State, 192 Ga. App. 820 (1989) (child molestation).

1991

2. Sims v. State*, 260 Ga. 782 (1991) (child molestation) [reversed].
3. Ross v. State, 199 Ga. App. 767 (1991) (burglary).
4. Jacobson v. State, 201 Ga. App. 749 (1991) (kidnapping).

1992

5. Martin v. State, 262 Ga. 312 (1992) (murder).

1993

6. Johnson v. State, 262 Ga. 716 (1993) (murder).
7. Norton v. State, 263 Ga. 448 (1993) (murder).

1994

8. Cost v. State, 263 Ga. 720 (1994) (murder).
9. Martin v. State, 211 Ga. App. 849 (1994) (drug possession).
10. State v. Crank, 212 Ga. App. 246 (1994) (drug possession).
11. Anderson v. State, 212 Ga. App. 329 (1994) (probation revocation) [reversed].
12. State v. Peters*, 213 Ga. App. 352 (1994) (murder).
13. Cost v. State, 264 Ga. 504 (1994) (murder).
14. McKnight v. State, 215 Ga. App. 899 (1994) (drug sale) [reversed].

1995

15. Grier v. State, 217 Ga. App. 409 (1995) (drug possession).
16. Tinker v. State, 218 Ga. App. 792 (1995) (RICO).

1996

17. Smith v. State, 266 Ga. 208 (1996) (murder).
18. Campbell v. State, 221 Ga. App. 135 (1996) (child molestation).
19. Campbell v. State, A95A2562 (1/11/1996) (armed robbery).

1997

20. McGarity v. State, 224 Ga. App. 302 (1997) (child molestation).
21. Mathis v. State, 224 Ga. App. 521 (1997) (armed robbery).
22. Parham v. State, A97A2117 (9/25/1997) (solicitation to commit murder).

1998

23. Clay v. State, 232 Ga. App. 656 (1998) (armed robbery).

24. Hillman v. State*, 232 Ga. App. 741 (1998) (feticide) [reversed].

25. Ramey v. State, 235 Ga. App. 690 (1998) (kidnapping).

1999

26. Terrell v. State*, 271 Ga. 783 (1999) (murder, death penalty sought) [reversed].

2000

27. Bracewell v. State, 243 Ga. App. 792 (2000) (manslaughter) [reversed].

28. Moody v. State, 244 Ga. App. 214 (2000) (armed robbery).

29. Davis v. State, 244 Ga. App. 345 (2000) (armed robbery).

30. Anderson v. State, 244 Ga. App. 643(2000) (armed robbery).

2001

31. Croy v. State, 247 Ga. App. 654 (2001) (child molestation).

32. Palmer v. State, 248 Ga. App. 515 (2001) (child molestation).

33. Brown v. State, 274 Ga. 202 (2001) (murder).

34. Roseberry v. State*, 274 Ga. 301 (2001) (murder).

35. Smith v. State, A01A1341 (8/31/2001) (kidnapping).

2002

36. Durden v. State, 274 Ga. 868 (2002) (murder).

37. Wormley v. State, 255 Ga. App. 347 (2002) (child molestation).

38. Bridges v. State, 256 Ga. App. 355 (2002) (escape).

39. Horner v. State, 257 Ga. App. 12 (2002) (motor vehicle theft).

40. Terrell v. State*, 276 Ga. 34 (2002) (murder, death penalty).

2003

41. Manuel v. State, 276 Ga. 676 (2003) (murder).
42. Simmons v. State, 262 Ga. App. 164 (2003) (aggravated assault).
43. Sparks v. State, 277 Ga. 72 (2003) (murder).

2004

44. Phelps v. State, 278 Ga. 402 (2004) (murder).

2010

45. Walsh v. State, A10A2119 (10/20/2010) (child molestation)

2011

46. Walsh v. State, S11C0687 (5/16/11) (cert. dismissed) (child molestation).